Words of Fire, Spirit of Grace

Words of Fire, Spirit of Grace

by

R. Grace Imathiu

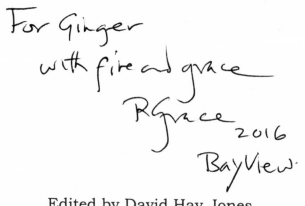

For Ginger
with fire and grace
R Grace
2016
Bay View.

Edited by David Hay Jones

Foreword by Bishop
Sharon Zimmerman Rader

True North
Porjus, Sweden & Milwaukee, U.S.

"Words of Fire, Spirit of Grace"
Published by True North, Porjus, Sweden and Brown Deer, Milwaukee, U.S.

Copyright by True North. Published 2003. Printed in the
United States of America.

ISBN 978-0-9720841-0-9

Contact the publisher, editor and author at "True North, Box 65,
982 60 Porjus, Sweden".

Send email to dhayjones@yahoo.com, g47@mailcity.com, yourgrace@lycos.com.

True North and the Rev. R. Grace Imathiu are
on the web at www.worksofgrace.org

Unless otherwise stated, Bible quotations are from
the Holy Bible New Revised Standard Version,
published by Zondervan Publishing House, 1989.

Cover photograph: Raindrop about to fall from a
pine needle, Lapland, Sweden, by
David Hay Jones of the Science Photo Library.

Dedicated to the memory of my friend
The Reverend O.B. Smith
(1908–2002)

"You are accepted by that which is greater than you...Simply
accept the fact that you are accepted."
(Paul Tillich)

How to read this book

This book puts Bible scholarship in the pulpit.

The contents page gives the complete Scripture text on which each sermon is based. Before reading the sermons, it is always helpful to read the relevant Scripture first. Read more than once if you find the Scripture text difficult to understand.

In each case, the Bible text is a departure point, and the sermon is an interpretation of the text, shining a light upon our lives and dreams, our frustrations and hopes. The sermons interweave interpretation with African folk stories, current world events and references to our daily lives.

The snippets of Bible text at the start of each chapter are intended as tasters. For the full text, always consult the contents page. These will tell you where to begin and end reading each passage so that you can fully follow the sermon.

The Bible text is living: it is about us today. As we read the Scriptures, the Scriptures in turn read us. Take your time, read and enjoy.

R. Grace Imathiu
Meru, Kenya

Contents

Editor's Note

Awake, O north wind, and come, O south wind! Blow upon my garden (Song of Solomon 4:16)

During the past two years, the time it has taken to work on this book, the world has been turned upside down. We have witnessed the attacks on the Twin Towers and the Pentagon, followed by the war and unsteady peace in Iraq. Only yesterday, I received the awful news that the Swedish foreign minister Anna Lindh had been stabbed to death while shopping in Stockholm, Sweden.

At such times, we long for news, reports and commentary which do more than spit the headlines at us in sound-bite form. Unfortunately, the rise of cable and 24-hour news broadcasting has led to an increase in the number of up-to-the-minute reports at the expense of analysis and critical commentary. And sadly, much of the new journalism is fiercely partisan, loud and bullying, with nothing to offer the friends of quiet reflection.

There are still places which value debate, depth of thought and analysis, which dare to ask challenging questions. At its best, church is such a place and within the best churches, the preacher is the key figure. When church goes beyond its traditional role as moral instructor and encourages open debate and discussion, when it tackles important ideas, it can be one of the most stimulating and exciting environments. A good preacher inspires people and gives them a glimpse of possibilities and opportunities they have never dreamed about. Grace Imathiu is one of those great preachers who can make us think, who can even make us laugh while we are thinking. She knows how to tell a story. She is one of a small number of world-renowned Methodist preachers and, as far as I know, she is the only African, woman preacher and Bible scholar with access to a world stage. Grace is as comfortable preaching to thousands at a stadium in Rio de Janeiro or London as she is in her small local church in Meru, Kenya.

When considered against this background, it is surprising that a big, international publishing house has not yet snapped her up and enabled millions of readers to access her profound, moving and humorous words. Part of the answer lies in Grace's refusal to behave like a celebrity or to swallow the myths of notoriety. Grace is not shallow. She does not sugarcoat her message and her perspective is always international, always looking beyond the safe and familiar.

Although her words reach the highest planes of our imaginations and seep into otherwise locked areas of our minds, Grace's feet are firmly planted on the ground. She knows what the world looks like. She is not only familiar with its affluent corners, its gated communites and manicured lawns, she knows, too, that millions and millions of God's children live in poverty, desperation and hopelessness.

She knows that many innocent children are victims of violence and that many dare not dream because the basics of life are denied them. And when, like Grace, you know the stench of poverty and have sensed the indefensible unfairness of abundance for the few and misery for the many, you cannot accept raw and brutal materialism as a sensible answer to anything. In all our comfort and smugness, Grace can make us uncomfortable. She opens our eyes to a world which is far from perfect and she urges us to act.

Grace also has the rare ability to communicate and connect with the unchurched. This is a gift at a time when millions of people, particularly in the western world, are questioning the church's relevance to modern life. Sermons which simply address the choir, which preach to the converted, have little role in broadening people's understanding of the Christian message and its relevance to all our lives. Grace makes the message mean something; it addresses us, engages us, speaks our language.

Grace speaks across barriers of class, gender and race. She avoids cheap points, never ingratiates herself with one group of people by mocking another. She is a woman of great integrity. She lives and breathes what she preaches, giving time to anyone who seeks her out. Although she could no doubt make a fine living by traveling the world fulltime, she likes to be grounded in the day-to-day work of serving a church and congregation. As a pastor, she has served in Kenya, Ohio, Tennessee and Wisconsin. She has just accepted an invitation to serve as senior pastor of Brown Deer United Methodist Church near Milwaukee.

My role in Grace's ministry has been to take on the welcome task of transcribing and publishing her sermons. Has it been easy? No. As soon as I started the work, I found out that there is a huge difference between the oral delivery of sermons and how they sound in one's head as read text.

A preached sermon can be up-to-the minute in its relevance and reference to people and places. But some humorous remarks have a very short shelflife and a narrow frame of reference, which might only make sense at one gathering. The following week, the references which seemed so pertinent can be outdated and irrelevant. This has had to be taken into account in the editing, and in a small number of cases Grace has had to rewrite or update her original sermon text. Where a remark risked falling flat or being misunderstood, it has been left out.

There are also a number of what can be called rhetorical devices which work brilliantly when delivered to an audience but which might strike a reader as odd. For example, preachers often like to employ repetition to hammer home a point. In order to encourage the audience to taste the words being used, to see them from different aspects, a word might be repeated three, four, five or more times. In text, when a word is repeated three or more times in a row it can at worst cause a reader to suspect a proofreading error.

There is also the question of taste and culture. I am cautious—a minimalist—preferring one word rather than two if I think it will do the job. Others, of a different taste, prefer verbal pyrotechnics; they like to see and hear evidence of a preacher's vast vocabulary. I have often heard preachers applauded for delivering a word or idea followed by ten or more synonyms. Where there have been small differences of opinion in such matters, I have chosen Grace's preference rather than my own.

In matters of style and usage, I have used three books: "The New York Times Manual of Style and Usage" published by Three Rivers Press; "The Oxford Dictionary of American Usage and Style" by Oxford University Press; and "The Elements of Style" by Macmillan & Co. These have helped to solve tricky questions of grammar, spelling, punctuation and consistency. We have also used the usage manuals to eliminate participle danglers, flotsam phrases and misplaced modifiers. In the few cases where Grace has disagreed with the manuals, I have used her wording. If any vestiges of British English remain, it is my fault and mine alone.

Finally, this book would not have been possible without the generous support and encouragement of Phil and Betsy Hendrickson, whom I thank for their patience, graciousness and unflinching enthusiasm.

I hope you all enjoy reading these sermons as I much as I have enjoyed listening to them, transcribing them and preparing them for publication.

David Hay Jones
Porjus, Lapland, Sweden

Foreword

In 2000, I appointed the Rev. Grace Imathiu, a clergy member of the Methodist Church in Kenya, to be the lead pastor of Green Bay First United Methodist Church. The appointment startled many, including Grace's father, Bishop Lawi Imathiu, who quietly inquired of me a year or so later, "What was going through your head when you asked Grace to go to First Church?"

Grace did not fit the preconceived notions of who the lead pastor would be in the land of the Green Bay Packers. She was a woman. She was still in the process of completing her work for a Ph.D. degree. She was not a member of the Wisconsin Annual Conference. She had not spent many years as a local church pastor. She was an African woman entering into a predominantly white congregation and community. But Grace could preach. And when Grace preaches, people listen and are changed. Perceptions about the world in which we live, about the Scriptures, and about God's claim on the life of individuals and the community are challenged and transformed.

Grace Imathiu evidences the best in preaching for the twenty-first century. She is a lover of the Scriptures, immersing herself in listening to the text, allowing the ancient story to speak once again to today's context and a particular culture. She engages in dialogue with the Scripture asking it questions, "worrying" it, challenging assumptions about it, always respecting it, and finally allowing it to speak for itself.

Grace knows that the preacher who opens herself to experience fully the Scripture's message and then invites others into that experience as well is engaging in a risky, sometimes frightening, and potentially shocking experience.

Preaching is an art, needing constant tending, practice and renewal. For me, preaching always begins and ends in the ancient story found in the holy Scriptures. But there are other stories as well. Grace Imathiu is an insatiable gatherer of life stories: given a particular text or theme with which to work, she has been known to send out requests for stories to assist her in developing a sermon or study. She opens herself to the reflections, suggestions and corrections of others. That dialogue and response are usually plain in Grace's sermons. The hearer is aware the sermon is not one individual's work alone and because it is not just Grace's solo work, the hearer feels invited to participate in the Good News that is being proclaimed.

Some will ask, "Why bother with another book of sermons?" This collection of Grace Imathiu's sermons will bless any reader, whether weekly Sunday preacher, lay member of a congregation, or inquirer about faith, as she illuminates the scriptural texts. You will delight in her creativity. You will be surprised by the twists, turns and scope of her storytelling. You will wonder at the challenge which comes to you. May God's yearning to be in touch with all of us be made plain and strengthened through the reading, reflection upon and strengthening which comes through the "Words of Fire, Spirit of Grace".

Sharon Zimmerman Rader, Bishop,
Wisconsin Conference, United Methodist Church

Words of Fire, Spirit of Grace

by

R. Grace Imathiu

Sermon Venues

The sermons in this book have been preached at venues all over the world. Some of the sermons have been delivered at more than one location.

1

Choosing to be Human

His disciples asked him, "Who sinned, this man or his parents, that he was born blind?" Jesus answered, "Neither this man nor his parents sinned; he was born so that God's works might be revealed in him." (John 9:2-3)

In an entire chapter of John's Gospel, the healing of a man who was born blind is described in great detail. The story is told in a way that cannot fail to amuse the reader. Who does not blink in amazement as the blind man, with mud and saliva on his eyes, makes his way to a specific and particular pool? Who does not chuckle as the village folk fail to recognize the man whose sight is now restored, saying they identified him only through his blindness and begging? Indeed, even the blind man's parents are amusing as they emphatically deny having anything to do with their son's restored sight. As the story unravels, perhaps John wants us to wonder who is blind: the disciples, the religious leaders or the community itself?

John begins the story as Jesus is walking along and the disciples see the man who was born blind. The blind man's predicament sparks off an intense debate and discussion among the disciples, who are curious as to the theological reason for the man's blindness: is it the result of his sin or had his parents sinned? Jesus refuses to be drawn into this discussion. He shifts attention from the blind man to God. For Jesus, this is not an occasion for theological speculations or ethical and philosophical arguments about blame, but an opportunity for God's action. Jesus heals the man.

This healing story challenges me. Although I am a disciple of Jesus who strives always to do as Jesus does, I must admit that I more often than not find myself enjoying the company of the disciples and am taken up with their discussions. More often than not, I am interested in knowing, "Who's fault is it? Who is responsible for this situation? Who is to blame for this man's blindness: the man, his parents, his community or society?" For instance, when I encounter a bigot who believes some nonsense about one group's superiority over another, I ponder and wonder and reflect on the cause of such bigotry? Is the individual wholly responsible for his or her bigoted beliefs or are we justified in blaming tribal myths? Is the media responsible? And what if someone is blind to the humanity of others or is ignorant of how their lifestyle or words destroy people's lives. Who is at fault for this? Where does individual responsibility begin and end? How wide is the grey zone of contention between individual and collective, or social, responsibility?

Jesus moves past such discussions. In his encounter with the man who was born blind, Jesus does the work of restoration, the work of bringing light into the man's world. The stakes are high in this healing. The details reveal that the man's condition is more than one of faulty eyesight. He was born blind. He has no sight and he has never had sight. No wonder the method of healing that Jesus employs is quite different from any method he had used elsewhere.

He spits on the ground, and in an action that calls to remembrance the work of God laboring on a lump of clay in Genesis 2:7, Jesus makes mud and places it on the blind man's eyes. It is as though Jesus makes new eyes for the blind man who was born without eyes. It is as though he makes something out of nothing. Yet the story is quite different from the Genesis story. You see, Jesus is not alone in recreating the blind man. He invites the blind man to participate in his own healing and restoration, instructing him, "Go, wash in the pool of Siloam." Can you see him? In my mind's eye I can see the blind man with mud on his face heading to the pool of Siloam. I see him, perhaps with his cane tapping his way across town. I see him asking for directions at the grocery store; perhaps a kind soul helps him along, perhaps a group of children follows him. With balls of mud on your face and such hope in your voice, you would surely draw attention to yourself.

He went, he washed, and behold. Sight! That is his testimony. But so different was he from the blind beggar the town knew that they hardly recognized him. The neighbors think it cannot possibly be him. They think he must have a twin. This happens, you know. When spiritual eyes are opened, not only does one see differently, one looks different. Behold a new creation! As if his ability to see made him appear different to people who had known him. My goodness! Maybe, after all, appearance is not skin deep, does not have to hinge on a facelift or a nose job. How you look has a lot to do with how you see and feel.

The blind man with his eyes restored never had such a hard time in his life. Seeing was trouble. It turns out he had been healed on a sabbath day and rules had been broken. Turns out, the prosecution wanted him to testify that Jesus was a sinner. Turns out, his entire family was dragged into the mess. And it turns out that this man, who had once been blind, had no clue who Jesus was. Face to face with Jesus, Jesus asks him, "Do you believe in the Son of Man?" Baffled, the man can only ask, "And who is he, sir? Tell me, so that I may believe in him "

Son of Man. Of all Jesus' identities, none is more complicated and messy in church history than Jesus as the Son of Man. But Son of Man is Jesus' own favorite title for himself. Jesus calls himself Son of Man numerous times in the Gospels. No one else calls him by that name. The voice from heaven calls him Son of God. The rich young ruler calls him teacher. Peter calls him Messiah. The lepers call him Master. Some call him Lord and others call him Son of David. In the

Gospels we encounter name after name for Jesus, title after title, but Jesus identifies himself as Son of Man.

What exactly does the title mean? Simple, Son of Man means "human being" or "human one" or "mortal". There is nothing special about it. Nothing exotic. In a basic sense, each one of us is a son of man. We are human beings, we are mortals. The term is not unique to Jesus. Jesus did not coin the term. The Psalms have it, the books of Daniel (7:13) and Ezekiel (2:1-6) have it, First Enoch (37-91) has it. To be a "Son of Man" is to be human, like all of us.

But what a problem the church has had with this term in our history. For instance in the first century, Christians like you and me began to be uncomfortable with the idea of Jesus as a human being. They were comfortable with Jesus as the Son of God, but Son of Man just didn't do it for them.

The problem was Christological. They wondered whether Jesus could be truly human if he was also truly divine? Poring over the Scriptures one can clearly see the humanity of Jesus because he gets hungry, gets thirsty, gets tired. When his friend dies, he weeps. When he finds the temple operating like a market, he loses his cool. Pore over the Gospels and we can see that Jesus has very human emotions. He is just like us, a fellow Son of Man.

And yet in what sense is he human when we know that he is also the Son of God? Look! He walks on water, he is not like us. He is not like us because he knows our innermost thoughts and is impossible to deceive. He is Son of God. And yet he is so like us, a Son of Man.

The attempt to reconcile Jesus' divinity with his humanity has proven too confusing for many in our Christian family. Some have wondered whether Jesus suffered on the cross. Can God suffer? Can God feel pain? On a scale of 1 to 100, how human was Jesus? The folks named Docetics decided that Jesus was not really human. They decided he was 100 percent divine and when he seemed human, he only "appeared" to be human. They decided that God could not experience pain as a human does, so God was only pretending to be one of us.

4

The Docetic explanation does not suffice for Christians because we as a people of faith profess that in Jesus of Nazareth, God became truly and fully human. Jesus was tested in all the ways that we are but he was without sin. The Docetics could not accept this and were thrown out of Christianity. Their beliefs were labeled heretical.

Jesus is human, he loves being human. Time and time again he calls himself human: Son of Man. And he came to teach us how to be human: Son of Man. You see, Jesus is the new beginning. Jesus is the new Adam. Jesus came to show us how God intended for us to be. When we were created in God's image, male and female, God saw it was good to be Son of Man. Jesus is the perfect human being. God had Jesus in mind while laboring on a lump of clay making you and me and announced to all "it is good!" Son of Man!

For those who have been taught merely to survive, Jesus comes to teach us how to live deeply as human beings, how to be that which God created in God's image. Go ahead, learn how to be unashamedly human. It might be just what you need in order to laugh and love and lead a fulfilled life on planet earth.

In his encounter with a blind man, Jesus shows us how to be the kind of people God made us to be. Jesus moves past the disciple discussions, beyond apportioning blame. Jesus' attention shifts from scapegoating and blame and instead points to God. The blind man's condition is an opportunity for God's goodness. This an opportunity for mercy. This is one opportunity when meanness does not have the last word.

2

Our Elephant

For just as the body is one and has many members, and all the members of the body, though many, are one body, so it is with Christ. For in the one Spirit we were all baptized into one body – Jews or Greeks, slaves or free – and we were all made to drink of the one Spirit. Indeed, the body does not consist of one member but of many. If the foot would say, "Because I am not a hand, I do not belong to the body," that would not make it any less a part of the body. And if the ear would say, "Because I am not an eye, I do not belong to the body," that would not make it any less a part of the body. If the whole body were an eye, where would the hearing be? If the whole body were hearing, where would the sense of smell be? But as it is, God arranged the members in the body, each one of them, as God chose. (1 Corinthians 12:12-18)

When I was in first grade, I heard my father tell a story which is aptly entitled "Our Elephant". Suddenly I understood. I grasped how the church works with its many members who make up the one body of Christ.

"Our Elephant" is a simple tale of a man who goes hunting in the forest and shoots down an elephant with his bow and arrow. He is so glad: imagine all that meat. He will not need to hunt for months on end. But there remains the daunting and demanding task of dragging the elephant back to his hut. Determined, he grabs the animal by one leg and pulls, attempting to budge the massive carcass, but the animal won't shift, it's far too heavy for one man to pull. He tries to haul it by the trunk; he pulls and strains, pulls and strains but the elephant won't budge. By the tail....same thing; the elephant is too darn heavy.

Finally the elephant hunter goes to his village and announces he has killed an elephant and needs help to drag it back to his hut. The villagers listen and one of them asks, "Whose elephant is it?"

"Mine, of course," replies the hunter.

"If it is your elephant," the villager says, "it is your problem. Pull it home yourself".

As the villagers begin to leave and return to their homes, the hunter rethinks the problem and announces: "I have killed the elephant for all of us". The villagers stop in their tracks. "An elephant for all of us? Our elephant?"

They break into celebration and quickly gather and troop off enthusiastically to the forest to find the slain elephant. Men, women, children, everybody joins in, determined to drag the elephant back to the village. Even the aged and frail join the crowd, insisting that if they cannot help drag the elephant, they will cheer on the work.

In the forest, gathered around the huge animal, the villagers each grab a piece of hide. And somebody begins to shout, "One, two, three, whose elephant?" And the villagers reply in unison, "Our elephant," pulling as they do so. Again, "One, two, three, whose elephant?" And they shout their reply, "Our elephant," shifting the huge animal a few more inches closer to home.

As they near the village they notice that when someone shouts "Whose elephant?", the hunter's lips do not quite match the words of "Our elephant." So one by one the villagers pause and when someone again shouts "Whose elephant?", they listen for the hunter's response. What a surprise to hear him muttering "My elephant."

So they leave the elephant right there and it takes a whole day and night of begging and promising by the hunter that it was "Our elephant" before they return to pull the elephant back to the village again.

This elephant story hits close to home for me. In our family tree, my great-great-grandmother was among the first persons in our family to go to church. Her name was Gake. Everybody called her Gake. Her parents called her Gake. Even her husband called her Gake. This was quite strange because Gake simply means "Auntie". She was everybody's Auntie. To this day, even my grandmother does not know her own mother's real name. She too calls her Gake.

Our family has discussed this subject long and hard and we have decided that Gake came to be called Gake, or Auntie, because of her interest in everybody's business. She was not a gossip, it's just that she knew the business of everyone in the village. She was a one-woman library, a living archive, the village historian, the Reuters news servive of Meru. She was the original search engine.

And when construction started on the first church in her village, when the first mound of earth was moved to level the ground, Gake was there. It was her business to be there. For the entire week as the church was pieced together from sticks and mud and a grass thatch, Gake would come to the site to carry this and carry that and all the while she would ask questions.

At the very first service, Gake was the very first person in church and she seated herself right in the middle of the proceedings in order to follow what was happening around her. Gake was always in the midst of things. She watched like a hawk as the minister, a young Englishman, fresh off the boat from England, began the service. She followed the singing and prayers and reading of Scripture. All went well until the minister and his translator stood up to preach. After a few minutes of stop-and-start preaching, first in English, then in Kimeru, Gake could stand it no more.

She announced in a loud voice, "Young man, sit down, I will take it from here. I know what you are trying to say, I know these people inside out, I will preach instead, I will tell them what you are trying to say." And she began to preach, and if anyone fidgeted or made to leave, Gake would call them out by their name and say, "You had better sit down or I will tell these folks about you-know-what..." Nobody dared leave. The congregation was trapped. Gake preached and preached; she preached from ten o'clock that morning until three in the afternoon. She quit only because she lost her voice and could speak no more. The English minister was dumbfounded; he had not seen anything like it. He was a prim and proper Englishman and people simply did not do things in that manner where he came from. He was not at all happy. He might even have said that he was "jolly annoyed".

Come Monday morning, the minister paid Gake a visit and told her in no uncertain terms never to speak in church again. She listened in astonishment, hardly believing what she was hearing. To cut the story short, the young man was telling her, "The church is my elephant and mine alone".

Gake listened politely a little while longer and then asked the minister, "Are you saying that you and only you are the one that knows God? Are you the one that brought God here? Hasn't God always been here among us? Are you the only one who can talk about God while the rest of us are supposed to sit quietly like a pile of firewood waiting to be tossed onto the fire?" And Gake never set foot in church again, never talked about church again. Gake's first time in church was her last time.

I never met Gake; she was dead many years before I was born but I know so many stories about her that I feel I know who she was. And throughout my ministry I have thought and rethought the Gake story over and over again. I have tried to figure out why the minister got so angry with her. Was he threatened by this mere five feet zero inch woman who did not know a word of English and who had never journeyed farther than 50 miles from her home?

Was the minister unable to see Gake as a co-worker in ministry, as a partner in God's work? Was the pastor not able to think it through for himself and conclude, "Thanks be to God who always goes ahead of us in our ministry. God has provided me with an evangelist who knows the local language and who knows the people. On Monday I am going to visit her and teach her and equip her and train her so she can be a better evangelist."

Somebody should have told that minister the "Our Elephant" story. Now here I am, nearly 93 years after that incident, and I am a minister. And I have often had conversations in my head with Gake. I tell her, "If ever I come to a church where a person such as you is present, I will welcome your every word, celebrate your gifts. I will thank God for your boldness and enthusiasm. Our church would train and equip you and fine tune your gifts. I am glad that people like you Gake wish to attend church. I am glad you want to help pull our elephant."

I am a minister with a congregation full of talented and enthusiastic members. On any given week our church is a hub of activity. If Auntie had been in church this past week, I would have taken her through the work that goes on in every office and meeting room. I would have shown her the many small groups where she would have met fellowship and laughter and tears and studying of the Bible and praying. I would have taken her to the trustee meeting where the Christian insurance salesman, the Christian lawyer, the Christian interior decorator and the Christian carpenter sit around the same table.

I would have taken her to the finance committee meeting and she would have joined me around the table with fellow Christians who are MBAs and accountants, who know how to make financial projections and understand the budgets that are nothing but meaningless numbers to the untrained eye. I would have taken Auntie to history committee meetings where the members are passionate about preserving our church documents and records.

I would have said to her, "Look around this table and see how God has called experts in business and finance, interior decorators, electricians, lawyers and homemakers and see how each one brings his or her know-how so that God's house will always be financed and

11

furnished, repaired, maintained and in beautiful order". She would have seen how this big elephant had been pulled from forest to village.

This past week I would have taken Auntie through a church where we all pull together on "our elephant".

Sisters and brothers, every gift in this congregation has its own special niche. If you are not involved in a small group or a task force or a committee or a mission group or a prayer group or a letter-writing group or in ushering or evangelizing or teaching Sunday school or rocking babies in the nursery, then you need to get your hands on our elephant and pull.

Whose elephant? Our elephant!

3

Armed with Prayer

Then Jesus told them a parable about their need to pray always and not lose heart. He said, "In a certain city there was a judge who neither feared God nor had respect for people. In that city there was a widow who kept coming to him and saying, 'Grant me justice against my opponent.' For a while he refused; but later he said to himself, 'Though I have no fear of God and no respect for anyone, yet because this widow keeps bothering me, I will grant her justice, so that she may not wear me out by continually coming' " And the Lord said, "Listen to what the unjust judge says. And will not God grant justice to his chosen ones who cry to him day and night? Will he delay long in helping them? I tell you, he will quickly grant justice to them. And yet, when the Son of Man comes, will he find faith on earth?" (Luke 18:1-8)

I am truly baffled by the parable that Jesus told about the poor widow and the unjust judge. I have studied and scrutinized and scanned the parable and still I don't get it. I have looked at the original manuscripts in the original languages and my unease will not settle. I have read and re-read commentaries and essays and sermons on this parable and I am just as stumped as when I first met it. I don't know why, but this is an extremely tricky parable. No matter how I look at it, there are more questions than answers. So let me admit right away that this is one tough nut to crack. No wonder this parable is found only in the Gospel of Luke. The other Gospels, Matthew, Mark and John, don't have it. Don't ask me why. I only know I don't blame them. It's the kind of parable that could keep a reader wide awake late into the night, wondering...wondering... wondering.

Let's be brave. Instead of tossing this parable into the tip-toe-carefully-around-it box, what if we dare to trust God and engage the parable? What if we trust that the parable is deep and wide and strong enough to handle our questions and queries? You see, truth is, I have a hunch that we have a goldmine in this parable. I have a hunch that this is one of those treasures that stare you in the face. I have a hunch this parable is one of those keys which enable us to unlock a deep and wonderful mystery.

The parable is a very simple Jesus story. Like every Jesus story it is so simple even a child could understand it. There are only two characters and the storyline is your basic case of bad guy, good girl. The bad guy is really, really bad. He is a mean man and a mean judge with so much power that he runs an entire city and thinks he needs nobody, not even God. Jesus describes him as a man who "neither feared God nor had respect for people" (Luke 18:2). Lest one thinks Jesus is rather harsh and judgmental, the man says of himself, "I have no fear of God and no respect for anyone" (Luke 18:4). He is cold and rude and he knows it. He has power and he is accountable to no-one, not even to God and certainly not to the people. He thinks he needs no one.

This judge, this harsh man, encounters someone completely different from himself: a powerless woman who lives in the city. Setting the parable in a time and place where the best chances for a woman were to be associated with a man, her man is dead. She is a widow. As if that is not enough, she has legal problems with someone she calls "my opponent". We are not told what her problems are, nor who her opponent might be. For all we know, her woes might have been caused by landlord troubles or she might be the victim of a family dispute over her dead husband's property. Or perhaps someone owed her money and refused to pay. The bottom line is that she needs the assistance of the heartless judge. And knowing all we know about the judge, the case seems firmly closed before it opens.

Yet even under these desperate circumstances, the widow refuses to accept injustice as the last word. She refuses to lie down and die. She refuses to participate in her own victimization. Something in her hopes for a better day, even if it takes her entire lifetime to get there. Day in and day out, she does the one thing she can. She gets out of bed, walks out of her house, goes to the judge and asks for the one thing he can give her: justice. She does not ask the judge for kindness or understanding or love or even a hug. She asks him to do his job, to deliver justice. "Grant me justice, grant me justice, grant me justice," she pesters him day in, day out.

At first the judge is clearly not going to yield. In fact he refuses to grant her justice. He snubs her, ignores her and throws her case out of court without opening the file.

But the unjust judge underestimates the widow's commitment to her rightful due of justice. And she has tools with which to fight. What she lacks in power, she compensates for in tenacity. The judge cannot withstand the continuous pressure from this lone woman. He cannot bear to see and hear her in his every waking moment. All he wants is to get rid of her, but she wears him down. He throws up his hands in surrender and gives her the justice she seeks. What a shock it must have been both for her opponent and the entire city. Imagine a judge, who neither fears God nor respects other people, yielding to a powerless widow. It must have made the main headlines in that city's newspapers. She must have been invited to every talk show in the country after that incredible victory. She must have written a best-selling book. My goodness, what she had done was in the same category as growing carrots in the Sahara desert.

So Jesus tells the parable and he tells me that the parable is about prayer. That is how prayer works, says Jesus. And of course I am totally befuddled. It doesn't help at all that I have read and heard the many commentaries which argue that God is like the ruthless and powerful judge and we are the poor, powerless widow. Apparently, to get anything from God, we must wear God out with our prayers. The idea is to picket the gates of heaven with dogged determination, to be there day and night with our prayer request for healing or for a spouse or for a pay raise, until God is worn out and gives us whatever we are asking for.

Of course, that interpretation is completely wrong. There are some things we know for sure: God is very different from the mean judge. Unlike the judge, God has special concern for those who are in need. Read the Scriptures and you will find that God has already put in place a safety net of grace for the weak and powerless in society. Read the Scriptures and you will find there are laws laid down precisely because of God's special concern for the well-being of the widow, the orphan, the lame, the blind, the homeless, the refugee, the child, the elderly and the stranger. God is hardly like the judge of the parable. Unlike the judge, God does not need to be worn out by our begging for justice to be done. God is the exact opposite of the unjust judge.

I have been kept wide awake at night trying to figure out who is who in this parable. For the longest time I did not know what to think. But what if? What if God is the widow? Are you surprised? It took me forever to get there. I don't know why. Perhaps I had bypassed the widow because of her lack of power. Perhaps I had dismissed her because of her gender. And yet she is so much like God. Look at her, armed with nothing but persistence, armed not with power and might but constantly seeking justice. Oh yes, she certainly reminds of God who seeks us out even when we repeatedly give God "No" for an answer. But God does not give up on us, not even when we line up arguments against God, throwing out the case for God's love even before it hits our hearing. No, God does not quit on us. God seeks us out. At times it even looks like God is trying to grow carrots in the Sahara desert!

God never gives up on any of us. Over and over again there is the story of God seeking us out, going that extra mile. God who comes to live as one of us, among us. Even when it looks like the case is closed, God's love never falters, never runs out of steam. No wonder the apostle Paul gave witness of that love saying, "I am convinced that neither death, nor life, nor angels, nor rulers, nor things present, nor things to come, nor powers, nor height, nor depth, nor anything else in all creation, will be able to separate us from the love of God in Christ Jesus our Lord." (Romans 8:38-39).

So Jesus tells us this incredible parable. A story of the widow whose persistence was a form of resistance. She looked unarmed and powerless, but she was armed to the teeth. She did what none other could have done. Luke puts the parable in the context of prayer, telling us that the parable ought to teach us how to pray. And if God is the widow, prayer is certainly not asking God for stuff, for material things. To pray is to allow oneself to be as vulnerable as the widow. To pray is to open oneself to the Spirit of God. Asking that we might be more like God, to allow ourselves to be as vulnerable as the little baby in the manger in Bethlehem. To pray is to believe that the impossible is possible, to be persistent in seeking justice not just for ourselves, but for all God's children in all of God's world.

Hallelujah, Amen.

4

Rattrap in the House!

Then Jesus said, "There was a man who had two sons. The younger of them said to his father, 'Father, give me the share of the property that will belong to me.' So he divided his property between them. A few days later the younger son gathered all he had and traveled to a distant country, and there he squandered his property in dissolute living. When he had spent everything, a severe famine took place throughout that country, and he began to be in need. So he went and hired himself out to one of the citizens of that country, who sent him to his fields to feed the pigs. He would gladly have filled himself with the pods that the pigs were eating; and no one gave him anything. But when he came to himself he said, 'How many of my father's hired hands have bread enough and to spare, but here I am dying of hunger! I will get up and go to my father, and I will say to him, "Father, I have sinned against heaven and before you; I am no longer worthy to be called your son; treat me like one of your hired hands." ' (Luke 15:11-19)

Jesus once told a parable about a family. The parable began with a very simple "A man had two sons." Nothing extraordinary about that, nothing unusual, nothing particularly interesting. A simple story about

19

a man who had two sons, an ordinary family and to tell you the truth, nothing earth-shattering happens. Sons behave like sons often behave and the father behaves like the book on parenting says he should.

Yet scholars tell us that this very ordinary story is the best known and best loved of all parables. One scholar ventures to call this parable "Jesus' masterpiece". It moves even seasoned, stuffy and Greeked-out exegetes of the Bible. When writing about this parable, scholars sway from their scientific, value-free, objective approach and become remarkably tender. One exegete says this parable "is the most exquisite and pehetrating of all stories about divine mercy and love." Did you catch the adjectives? Exquisite. Penetrating. Divine.

And that great African ancestor of the Church, St. Augustine of Hippo, confesses that he was moved to tears by the story of the younger son. He writes in the "Confessions" that "This story is about me. I who had squandered the gifts of intelligence and quickness on being a word seller. I had squandered God's gifts on fruitless readings and unwholesome texts which I fed on but it was like feeding on husks of hogs. Instead of being nourished I became weaker." For Augustine, the parable strikes a tender chord. It is the story of his own conversion.

Surely it is amazing that such a familiar, simple, plain and basic story could have such a profound effect.

Our tradition has not done us any favors by giving the parable the popular title "The Parable of the Prodigal Son". The parable did not originally come with a title. And let it be noted, I have nothing against titles; they are often helpful. But titles can sometimes be harmful and even dangerous. Titles put a good story in a cage and mislead us into thinking that naming the thing tells us everything there is to know about it. Titles tend to domesticate and tame good stories until they become easy and mundane and impotent. Titles can make us lazy and complacent.

But a title cannot cage a parable. Parables are parables precisely because they cannot be managed or neatly packaged. Show me a managed parable and I will show you a dead parable!

Cameron Semmens writes great poetry. I have told Cameron that one of his poems is a good definition of a parable. It goes like this:

This poem is untitled.
This poem has no title.
This poem wants no title.
This poem rebels against any
appropriate, feasible and/or
logical title that you may happen to think of.
The first line of this poem
is not to be supplemented as a title.
It is not even to be referred to as:
"The Poem That is Untitled"
or "That Untitled Poem"
or "Untitled."
It is to have no name, heading
or abbreviated term or reference of any type.
And this poem upholds the God-given right
to remain untitled.
If it is ever to be referred to,
it is to be recited in its entirety
and read with all sincerity.
This poem is untitled
is never to be titled
and shall not ever have a title.
This poem also reserves the right to peter out.
(footnote: this poem is diminished not quite finished)

Jesus told a parable about a family. A parable without a title. But tradition has assigned the title "The Parable of the Prodigal Son", which has stuck even though it is hardly accurate. The title shifts attention from the family, and privileges one member as though the whole parable is solely about that member. But hang on! This is a Jesus parable, not a Hollywood production with room for only one star and everybody

21

else is supporting cast whose sole task is to throw light on the principal protagonist. Real families do not work in that way. Families are way more complex than titles.

In this story, the younger son decides to leave home. We are not told why he leaves, so there is plenty of room to speculate on the circumstances. We can attempt to glimpse below the surface, fill in the gaps and read between the lines. We are given plenty of room to theorize. Some of us might speculate that the younger son had an adventurous spirit. Maya Angelou writes that he was seeking the kind of company he could not get at home so he left, simple as that. Some of us might speculate that sibling rivalry played a major role. And there are others who read closely and note that the parable has no mother, no sisters, no daughters, no grandmothers; in other words this is a household without women and the macho intensity of the parable-family is so great it would be enough to drive anybody out!

Whatever your theory, the story itself does not spell out why the younger son left home. We know only that he left in a manner that reveals he was not planning to come back. He packed everything he owned and what he couldn't pack and take with him, he sold and put the denarii in his wallet. Imagine him withdrawing his savings, closing the account and tearing up his bank book. Then he has a talk with his old man and says, "Dad, it's like this: if there is anything that you were planning to leave me in your will, I'll take it now. For me, you are dead."

He sold whatever piece of his inheritance his father gave him and he put the shekels in his by now fat wallet. He was financially equipped to leave the familiar and venture into the unknown. But let us not judge the son too harshly. Let us dare to give him the benefit of the doubt and wish him luck as he goes off to some faraway land. He crosses borders and enters Gentile territory where folks are different in all ways; they even have pig farms and pork chops on the menu.

This story of leaving home is a familiar one for many of us who are born and brought up in locations that have been labeled the third world or developing or pre-industrialized nations. Many of us from Africa can connect immediately with this parable because so many of us have been more or less forcibly displaced, disconnected from our families, traditions and language. Even those of us who have traveled abroad by choice can feel alienated, misunderstood, invisible and unwanted. So many Africans have left home in pursuit of a dream glimpsed in magazines or the movies or through conversations with western visitors who perhaps exaggerate the affluence of their own countries and the ease with which anyone, even foreigners, can earn a living and carve out a new, fulfilling life for themselves.

And there are Africans who have left home because of a poverty that is brutal, indiscriminate and soul-destroying, where not even the most talented and hard working people are rewarded with enough to feed themselves. For others, war and conflict have forced them to flee from homes which they would not otherwise have left and to which they long to return.

It is a sad fact that for many people in our world, home means a place where governments have little or no respect for human rights, where torture and abuse are commonplace, where leaders grow rich while ordinary folks sink deeper into poverty and misery. In such conditions, many feel compelled to leave, even if it means shattering the fabric of their family lives and living for months on the run, in hiding or in refugee camps. Truth be told, this parable is about many of us in today's world. So let us not judge the younger son too harshly. Let us wish him well as he goes off to make his new life.

Yes, Jesus once told a parable about a family. The parable could easily have begun with the words "A woman had two sons" but the popular title "The Parable of the Prodigal Son" shifts the attention from the community called family and focuses on only one member. The traditional title makes the misleading assumption that the prodigal son's story and history is the only legitimate and sole history of the entire parable. The title implies that only one level of the story is important and overrides all the other stories and histories and descriptions, the many layers of the actual parable. In our world we see how this pans out so that the story of only one group of people, one race, one nation, one gender is written and read as the one and only legitimate history of the entire world.

Admittedly, I grew up not so much worrying about the misleading title but trying to figure out which of the two sons was "the prodigal." My friends and I argued until the cows came home about one which of the two sons was prodigal. Some say the younger son was the prodigal one. Others argue passionately it was the elder son. And of course there are those who say that both sons were prodigal.

With only the parable's lost-and-found literary neighborhood of "lost and found sheep", "lost and found coins" and my own language of Kimeru which calls this story "Rugono rwa mutana uria waurite" or "The story of the lost son," I have always assumed that prodigal meant lost. I have always thought the lost sheep was a prodigal sheep and the lost coin was a prodigal coin and anyone who has a poor sense of direction and is constantly lost is an example of prodigal.

But wait, the problem is easy to solve. We need wait no longer. Although I have never heard anybody use the word prodigal in any ordinary conversation, Webster's Dictionary gives us the meaning and clears up the matter once and for all. Oh dear! Prodigal has nothing to do with the lost and found department. Prodigal is not even a very bad thing to be. Webster's says prodigal means extravagant, reckless, profuse, squandering and wasteful. A prodigal person is a spendthrift. Prodigal also means abundant, bounteous and lavish. Out of prodigal comes prodigious.

People who are not prodigal are miserly, stingy, mean and tight-fisted. There is no doubt that when prodigal is inward-looking, it is sinful in its self-indulgence, greed and selfishness, like the young son and the elder son.

But look! When prodigal is practiced on another, prodigal is radical. Prodigal is reckless in its welcome, such as when a returning son is met by a father who drops whatever he is doing and runs across the public square: that is prodigal. Prodigal is overwhelming in its forgiveness, such as when a raggedy, battered, lived-with-swine-looking daughter is clasped and rocked in the loving arms of her mother who laughing and crying can only say over and over again, "Thank you Jesus!" That is prodigal.

Prodigal means excessive, too much, extravagant, overflowing, unconstrained, like a mother who forgets cultural codes and overjoyed falls on her son's neck, embracing him and kissing him. Prodigal is the reckless dishing out of heaped helpings of mercy, dishing out extravagant portions of love. Prodigal is doling out grace in squandering and wasteful servings.

So look and see the picture before us: nothing but the finest robe on his battered and bruised body; nothing but the most precious rings on a finger that is a stranger to manicures; the best shoes for dusty, calloused feet; let's barbecue the fatted calf because there is no better day we are saving it for. Call the musicians, let every one dance, dance, dance (Luke 15:22-23).

And now a toast. A prodigal, passionate toast: "Raise your glass one and all. A toast! Here is to resurrection! He was dead but is alive again!"

My friend Viki Matson puts it well when she says: "When the table is filled to overflowing, when kindness abounds, when love begets more love and generosity gives birth to forgiveness...those kinds of feasts can only come from a God who is amazing, open-hearted, extravagant and beyond comprehension."

Jesus once told a parable about a family. A simple story about a man and his two daughters. Jesus did not label the parable but simply told the story and let the chips fall where they would. Traditions and cultures and annual conferences do not particularly like chips flying about; they prefer some sort of order, things in their correct place. So the tradition of scholarship has helped Jesus some and given this parable the neat, smooth and yet highly dangerous label of "The Parable of the Prodigal Son". The label sells the parable short. While the parable is wonderfully complicated like the family called the church, the label oversimplifies the family. The label dangerously zooms in on only one family member at the cost of the entire household. The label allows us to shift attention from the complex dynamics of the household and instead privilege one member as the legitimate and sole point of the entire story. The label insists on some grand narrative history which is clear and coherent, and for the sake of this clarity and coherence, other characters in the parable are devalued, silenced and dismissed as nothing more than supporting actors. The traditional label is addictive because it allows us to safely sidestep the intricate nature of human character and the complexity of family and human relationships.

But with Jesus, there are no labels. Jesus simply told a story and said "An ancestor had two children." Hang on. Wait a minute. Only two children? For me, as an African, that can't be right. I cannot imagine any of my ancestors having only two children. Immediately we know this cannot possibly be an African story, this is not an African ancestor. In Africa, two children is too few. If it were a good African story the parable would give the ancestor 100 sons like the man who had 100 sheep or at least 10 daughters like the woman who had 10 coins. But an ancestor with only two children is very unusual.

Stories that carry only two children should be read with great care. Stories with only two children can easily be misquoted and mislead us into a deadly dichotomy of elder child versus younger child. Next thing we know, such a dichotomy bleeds over into us versus them, villains versus victims, rich versus poor, liberal versus conservative, confessing versus reconciling, black versus white, the West versus the rest. Labels. Labels. Labels.

The truth of the matter is that life is not neatly and tightly packaged into either-or boxes. People, like parables, are impossible to label, catalogue and shelve. Not even nations are politically homogeneous, not even families have members who are entirely identical or exactly opposite, not even tribes can duplicate members so that if you have met one Meru, you've met all Meru. History itself is not monolithic. There is no coherent and clear grand narrative. Out there are real histories and realities quite unlike our own. What a terrifying thought it is; how it complicates preaching.

How do we survive juxtaposing our histories with the histories of people who are not like us and do not want to be like us? How do we preach in a manner mindful of the layers of exploitation and struggles of different groups of people? How do we live out as a body not just for some but for all of God's children? This can only be done by telling the whole story, the whole truth and nothing but the truth. It means allowing others to tell their stories and learning to listen to other people's stories. This parable is about interrelatedness, how all of us are connected.

Which reminds me of an African story about a rat living in the walls of a farmer's house. One day as the rat was going about its ratty business, it peered through a hole in the wall and saw how the farmer and his wife were opening a package. The rat watched carefully to see what was in the package. Rat could hardly believe its eyes when the farmer and his wife produced a rattrap! Yes, A rattrap. In a panic, the rat called the council of farm animals and in a trembling voice told them the farmer had bought a rattrap. Over and over again he repeated, "There's a rattrap in the house!"

The cow listened, the goat and chicken listened. Chicken scratched around a bit and finally said, "Well Brother Rat, I am standing here thinking to myself, 'Rattrap in the house, so what?' I have never heard of a chicken getting caught in a rattrap. I do not see what this has to do with me; it's none of my business." And the chicken walked away.

The goat nodded at chicken's words but offered understanding and pity, saying, "Brother Rat, you take care now, we will be praying for you and remember, God loves you! You take care now, you hear!"

The cow chewed cud for a while thinking hard and finally said, "It's like, I am confused man, like why are we here? See what I'm saying? And it's like I'm thinking, you know, cows and like rats and I am like too big to fit in the trap, man, and I figure, duh, that trap's not for me, man," and the cow walked off.

That same night, late, late at night "Pap!" went the rattrap and suddenly there's a scream from the farmer's house. Pandemonium breaks out. A snake had crawled into the rattrap. The farmer's wife had reached over and the snake had bitten her. Farmer rushed his wife to hospital. Sad, sad story, the farmer's wife died.

Farmer came home in shock. And you know how it is; people in shock must always be given fresh chicken soup. The following day, neighbors and relatives gathered at the farmer's house to comfort him. Farmer gave permission for the goat to be slaughtered for dinner.

On the day of the funeral there were so many people and the only way to feed them was for the farmer to give permission for beef stew on rice to be served. And all because of a rattrap!

Sisters and brothers, if you hear of rattraps in the house, don't pause to wonder whether it has anything to do with you. The Holocaust? Rattrap in the house! Kosovo? Rattrap in the house! The massacres in Rwanda? Rattrap in the house! The shootings at Columbine High? Rattrap in the house! The murder of Matthew Sheppard? Rattrap in the house! The killing of James Byrd Jr.? Rattrap in the house! The shooting of Amadou Diallo? Rattrap in the house!

So Jesus once told a story about us. God's family. A parable without labels and titles, without an obvious sign telling us how to read the story. Whatever our background, whatever our tastes and affiliations, Jesus told the story and allowed each one of us to find our own meaning. Let those who have ears hear!

5

Lost Faith

Now faith is the assurance of things hoped for, the conviction of things not seen. Indeed, by faith we understand that the worlds were prepared by the word of God, so that what is seen was made from things that are not visible. (Hebrews 11:1-3)

It was a pastoral emergency and the only thing I could think of was the story of the three little pigs.

You can imagine my surprise and confusion one Sunday morning, a day we have made it a habit to eat with one another at the Lord's table, and that particular Sunday one of my favorite people was in the sound room working the audiovisual equipment. I, as is my habit after serving communion, was headed to the sound room with the bread and the cup.

The young man waiting there had been confirmed in the church and was an active youth member. As always when serving communion, my heart was stuck in my throat remembering Jesus, remembering the simple story that people cannot ever betray one another. Those eating the same bread are kin; it is how people become related to one another, by eating at the same table.

Inside the sound room I held out the bread to my friend and said,

"The body of the Lord broken for you". He held up his hand, shook his head and said, "No thank you." I was not sure what he meant; did he want gluten-free bread, was that the problem? So I offered again, "The body of the Lord broken for you," and he repeated, "No thank you."

To whom was he saying no? To God? To Jesus? To kinship with us? I said the first thing that came to mind: "Say what?"

"No thank you," he told me, "I do not take communion anymore."

"It is a gift," I said to him. "You cannot refuse communion. Didn't your mother teach you to accept gifts? At Christmas, even if you receive gifts you do not like, you accept them and later, when no one is watching, you return them to the store. Haven't you heard never to look a gift horse in the mouth? Out of common courtesy, you should take this gift. We need to talk about this after church. This is a pastoral emergency."

I met with him and I listened as he told me he had lost his faith. It started the way it usually starts with lost faith: the struggle with God and evil, the equation that asks how an omnipotent, omniscient God can allow innocent people to suffer. Why doesn't God intervene to prevent babies from starving and dying? If God is all-powerful, all-good, all-loving, why is evil ever-present? Perhaps God is not all-powerful. Perhaps God is not all-good. And perhaps, as my friend argued, there is no God at all.

He started talking about the concept of hell, which bothered him deeply. And as a result, he had fired God, rejected God. God was out of his life. In fact, he confessed, he had never once felt God's presence in his life. He said that God was silent and absent. And so my friend had decided to trek through life on his own, saying he would take the risk that God was not going to punish him. Intellectually he had reached the place where he believed that people who believed in God were lying to, or at best deceiving, themselves.

People, he argued, so desperately needed to believe in something greater than themselves that they had concocted the notion of God, and this had been passed down from generation to generation, and today people were afraid to question whether it was right or wrong. We believed what our parents believed, he continued. Church didn't even let us ask questions or let us disagree with what we had been told. It was all about social control, about keeping people in line and preventing them from thinking freely. My friend thought that this had gone to such extremes that people who innocently questioned the existence of God were ostracized.

Call me crazy, call me a very bad pastor but apart from "have mercy on some who are wavering" (Jude 1:22), I could not think of a Scripture verse which would help. I could think only of the three little pigs. I was thinking my good friend's spiritual house had been hit by a hurricane and that this had happened millions of times to millions of people, including myself. The first time it happened to me, I was a student in West Virginia; it was my first summer away from home and I was desperately homesick. I remember my chemistry professor Dr Capstack trying to comfort me. He said: "Grace, as you journey through life you will find new building blocks with which you must rebuild your spiritual life".

Some people don't know what to do with a building block; they try to squeeze it into a space on a crumbling structure. Others know that old houses are often beyond repair and must be razed to the ground before new ones can be built. Dr Capstack told me, "I hope you don't leave this school without a spiritual home. I hope that you begin to build a new home, a new identity, a new knowledge of God".

And, 15 years later, it was my task to begin helping my friend to see his spiritual crisis as an opportunity for growth, not anger, doubt and despair. I wanted him to know that he was allowed to ask questions. I wanted him to see that God was indeed real, speaking to us through the stuff of our daily lives, that disappointment lay ahead if you thought God spoke solely via the esoteric and arcane. Disappointment lay ahead if you expected God to dwell away from you on a mountaintop, in a cave, remote sanctuary or temple, or in a burning bush, or a cloistered community where silence is cultivated, solitude appreciated and abstinence the rule. No, God shows up in our ordinary, everyday lives; that is where God's presence is seen and felt.

The place to start looking for God is in the nursery, in the kitchen, on the playground, in the parking lot, at the checkout counter, or as you hold a frail body that was once your parent, that was once your strong and healthy mother or father. God shows up, the eternal mystery shows up when we are performing the routine and mundane acts of serving faithfully.

The tragedy is we too often miss the God moments, the redemptive moments. Perhaps we can blame popular culture, where any sign of dullness or hardship gives us permission to give up, walk away, try something else, even a new religion, hoping we'll find a quick fix, fast track, take-out, instant-whip spirituality: just add water and stir. Hey presto, you have a new meaningful life!

But being in deep relationship with God is hard work. It demands rolling up your sleeves, rebuilding, constant attention to detail. If you build a house of greed, it washes away when the rains of economic depression smash down; the house of power collapses when the political climate changes; the house of living for the moment flips off its foundations when life opens up to the mysteries of birth, suffering or death. That is why Jesus calls us to build a house that will withstand the rain, wind and storms of life.

Will your spiritual house stand firm if cancer knocks on the door? Will it withstand the death of a loved one or betrayal by the one you trusted most? Jesus does not call us to walk on water. He did that. He doesn't call us to change water into wine. He did that. Jesus doesn't call us to multiply fishes and loaves; he did that. Jesus does not call us to die on a cross; he did that. Jesus calls us to believe in God. He cannot do that for us. Jesus calls us to trust God. He cannot do that for us. Jesus calls us to love one another. He cannot do that for us.

We must have faith. But what is faith? It is, as Renita Weems says, when we keep building from the last time you heard from God to the next time you hear from God. What is faith? It is when you don't believe in God, you know that God believes in you. God will give you the building blocks but God cannot build your spiritual house for you. You have to do that yourself, through tears, through confusion. And the body of Christ reminds you that we will be praying for you all the while. And that is why we have lunch and dinner with God on a regular basis. Two things to remember: build on a rock and eat with God often. Amen.

6

Go Home!

Then they arrived at the country of the Gerasenes, which is opposite Galilee. As he stepped out on land, a man of the city who had demons met him. For a long time he had worn no clothes, and he did not live in a house but in the tombs. When he saw Jesus, he fell down before him and shouted at the top of his voice, "What have you to do with me, Jesus, Son of the Most High God? I beg you, do not torment me", for Jesus had commanded the unclean spirit to come out of the man. (For many times it had seized him; he was kept under guard and bound with chains and shackles, but he would break the bonds and be driven by the demon into the wilds.) Jesus then asked him, "What is your name?" He said, "Legion"; for many demons had entered him. They begged him not to order them to go back into the abyss.

Now there on the hillside a large herd of swine was feeding; and the demons begged Jesus to let them enter these. So he gave them permission. Then the demons came out of the man and entered the swine, and the herd rushed down the steep bank into the lake and was drowned.

When the swineherds saw what had happened, they ran off and told it in the city and in the country. Then people came out to see what had happened, and when they came to Jesus, they found the man from

33

whom the demons had gone sitting at the feet of Jesus, clothed and in his right mind. And they were afraid. Those who had seen it told them how the one who had been possessed by demons had been healed. Then all the people of the surrounding country of the Gerasenes asked Jesus to leave them; for they were seized with great fear. So he got into the boat and returned. The man from whom the demons had gone begged that he might be with him; but Jesus sent him away, saying, "Return to your home, and declare how much God has done for you." So he went away, proclaiming throughout the city how much Jesus had done for him. (Luke 8:26-39)

The encounter with a many-named, demon-possessed, graveyard-dweller is one of the gospels' most dramatic and gripping stories. Hear it once and you'll never forget it. No wonder that the story is told in all three synoptic gospels (Matthew, Mark and Luke). It might be that the first Christians remembered the story and told it often.

We are told of a life that spirals out of control, with nothing to chain it down, a life that turns against itself and causes itself pain. It is about living with the sense of being displaced, the pain of never being able to claim an identity. What a story! After all these years I still get caught up in the drama, still love the strangeness, still wonder about the ending.

If we read Luke's account, he begins with an arrival at a specific location. Listen: "Then they arrived at the country of the Gerasenes, which is opposite Galilee". The place where we have landed is on the other side of Galilee. Matthew and Luke tell us that it is on the other side of the sea. Luke tells us it is opposite Galilee, which is the place where the fishermen left their nets and followed Jesus. But opposite Galilee is different theological territory, a place where nobody leaves their fishing nets and follows a man they have never seen before.

In fact, in this country when a human being is restored, there is no rejoicing, no clapping of hands and shouting of praises to God.

Here, the inhabitants are suspicious when people are restored to their right mind. Restoration makes the Gerasene people nervous and afraid. This is a country where pigs come first and the number of pigs you own makes you somebody. Let's honk for pigs! Welcome to the country of the Gerasenes! The specific location has never been pinned down. You will not find it on the map and there is even confusion about the name of the place. Matthew calls it Gadarenes. Mark names it Gerasenes. Luke follows Mark and names it Gerasenes. Some manuscripts call it Gergenes. Scholars don't know what to call it. Some say this, some say that. So we can agree that scholars have no clue about the exact geographical location of this place. Some say it could be here and some say it could be there. The rest of the Bible is not very helpful either. Nowhere else in the entire Bible do we find even a passing mention of Gadarenes or Gerasenes.

What does this tell us? There is the obvious conclusion that the place is not mentioned because it is hardly visited. Not many people come to the place. It's not a tourist trap, not a Holy Land Malibu or Copacabana. And when you know the following story, you don't wonder why.

"As Jesus stepped out on land, a man of the city who had demons met him. For a long time he had worn no clothes, and he did not live in a house but in the tombs." In other words, the welcoming committee comprises a man who is naked as a jay bird. And if you are thinking he must be out of his mind, you are probably right. The story says the man has demons; he is possesed, driven from his family and friends into the tombs where he now camps out, not in a house but among the tombs. Demon-possesed into becoming a tomb-dweller. A living, walking man who makes his home in the very place which houses the dead. A living, walking, talking man who makes his home in a place that houses memories, a place where the only language is in the form of noiseless inscriptions commemorating great lives and great deeds in only a few words, inscriptions that recall better times long forgotten by the living. What a bizzare place to run into a walking, talking, breathing man. The man is physically displaced.

Today, we'd call this a horror story. The man has lost everything, even his name. He does not know what he is or who he is. What does it mean to live a nameless existence, to dwell on the periphery, on the edge? Imagine living among the tombs, living but being as good as dead. Living a life of balancing between life and death, between sanity and losing your mind.

Unclean. Unclean. Unclean. The man is unclean. He is matter out of place, inappropriate; he does not fit. Oh, there can be only a few things worse than being called matter out of place. There can be only a few things worse than being treated as matter out of place because you are black in a whitewashed world; matter out of place because you are female in a male-dominated world; matter out of place because you are poor in world that values little labels that announce how much you paid for your shirt and sweater and socks.

Unclean. Unclean. Unclean. Look but don't touch him. Don't let him touch you. Look and see the telltale marks around his ankles, his wrists, his neck. The man is marked by violence and struggle. See the marks left by the chains and shackles and fetters that had once bound him. We are told they had tried to restrain him, to subdue him. Not once but often. They had wrestled him down and chained him up. We are told he had wrenched the chains apart. He had broken the shackles into pieces. He had snapped the fetters like kindling. He was stronger than all of his captors put together. Nothing and nobody could subdue him. He was like an entire Roman army. Call him Legion.

"What is your name?" He said, "Legion". This man is an enemy to those around him and to himself. Time and time again he would turn against himself. He would take stones and drive them into his own flesh. He would cut himself and not stop. Did these self-inflicted wounds mean he loathed himself, that he wished himself dead? He was a man in pain who caused himself pain. Wailing so loud they would hear him in all the surrounding ten cities. Wails that would cut through the hustle and bustle of ordinary days. Screaming day in, day out. His weeping. His howling. His sorrowing like some wounded creature out in the cold with nowhere to go. Poor lonely lost soul. Without even a name to hold on to.

For us in Africa, in our postcolonial context, in our political and ethnic turmoil, and economic struggles, the story of the Legion-invaded man is our story. The story is about us. About our situation. About our lives. This story is about Rwanda, a country turned into a graveyard within weeks. Within one hundred days, 800,000 people were chopped up like firewood with Chinese-made machetes. Most of the people were hacked to death by their next-door neighbors. The crazy thing about Rwanda's tragedy is that 90 percent of Rwanda's population were baptized, confessing Christians. Yet something sinister took over, snapping the theological framework into kindling, and nobody could subdue the madness, just like the madman of the Gerasenes.

A 16-year-old Rwandan girl named Josephine survived the genocide and gave international reporters a tour of her dead village. She took them to the church where she had been baptized and whispered, "We will never come back to this church. It is a graveyard. The angels have left us."

In Africa we know what it is to be trampled over by Legion, to have everything you ever called your own taken away. Your land, your theology, your language, your culture and even your name. Too many people in Africa live painfully dead-end lives like that madman of Gerasenes.

When they came to Jesus, they found the man from whom the demons had departed sitting at the feet of Jesus, clothed and in his right mind. Thank God for the Gospel. We who preach the Gospel have put all our eggs in God's basket. We are now risking everything for the Gospel. We do not have an alternative plan just in case this does not work out. We have sold up everything we own, given up everything we ever had and are staking it on the Gospel.

African theologians and pastors can no longer afford to mimic Christians from other places. We've been there and done that and it did not work. The price was too high. We can no longer afford to be satisfied with congratulations from our Western sisters and brothers for maintaining the status quo. Too many lives have been wasted. We are now in the business of exorcising Legion, exorcising the demons of lies upon lies about ourselves and our neighbors, demons that have blinded us to the image of God imprinted in our own cultures, in our own languages and in the color of our skin. We are now taking the risk of trusting God. And see, the new things that God is doing among us, calling us out of the tombstones of nostalgia into dreaming of the future and how good it is going to be, calling us out of the tragic habit of maintaining the church of the present rather than building the church of the future, a church that takes life's complexity seriously and searches persistently for new ways, new structures, new concepts, new theologies, new language, new metaphors to speak directly, clearly and meaningfully about God. We have to get new wineskins for this new thing God is doing. There is no way the old skins can hold the new wine! The excitement is sometimes overwhelming when we catch a glimpse of God's church of the future, where the Gospel runs deeper than the bones of our differences.

"Then all the people of the surrounding country of the Gerasenes asked Jesus to leave them; for they were seized with great fear". Jesus sent the healed tomb-dweller away, saying, "Return to your home, and declare how much God has done for you." The no-longer mad man was sent home by Jesus. He did not want to go home but that is where he was sent. He wanted to travel with Jesus, healing the sick, restoring sight and hearing to the blind and deaf, multiplying loaves and fishes and feeding five thousand. He probably wanted to be a part of that exciting disciple life but Jesus sent him home.

Go home and declare. Go home. Home: the toughest of all mission fields. Home, where everybody thought they knew him and nobody knew him. Home, where everybody was equipped with the ability to press the buttons that could lead him to lose his sanity again. Home. Go home to your friends. Home to your family. Go home and declare!

38

Can you see him going home? Can you visualize the villagers watching him? The anxiety as word spreads through the village about the man they knew as mad, howling, self-destructive, a tomb-dweller looking for a room to rent. He has come down from the hills and is looking for a job. Lord help us all. He is planning to live here. Imagine the curiosity, the security alert. He walks into the village fully clothed and in his right mind, knowing his name. And he is no longer howling.

He hums "Amazing Grace how sweet the sound that saved a wretch like me. I once was lost but now I am found, was blind but now I see." Yes, that is the song he hums! The song written by a former slave-trader years ago. The man is changed. After years of legion occupation, people can change.

The villagers are bewildered and look at each other wondering, "Is there something greater than Legion? Is there medicine for the madness?" His friends cautiously approach him, just a nervous handshake; he hasn't taken a bath yet. They look at him curiously, closely, missing nothing, noting the scars and ask him, "What happened? What really happened? We heard about the pigs! It's a wonder your affliction did not kill you."

7

Unpacking Privilege

Then Joseph could no longer control himself before all those who stood by him, and he cried out, "Send everyone away from me." So no one stayed with him when Joseph made himself known to his brothers. And he wept so loudly that the Egyptians heard it, and the household of Pharaoh heard it. Joseph said to his brothers, "I am Joseph. Is my father still alive?" But his brothers could not answer him, so dismayed were they at his presence. Then Joseph said to his brothers, "Come close to me." And they came closer. He said, "I am your brother, Joseph, whom you sold into Egypt." (Genesis 45:1-4)

Jacob, who later changed his name to Israel, had 12 sons, which is how we get the 12 tribes of Israel. The story goes that of all his 12 sons, Jacob loved his youngest son Joseph the dreamer best. To show how special this youngest son was to him, Jacob gave Joseph a special coat. The text says the coat had long sleeves but the popular interpretation, a coat with many colors, grabs the imagination. And we can't complain: the "technicolor coat" has landed Joseph on Broadway.

Jacob's favoritism does not go unnoticed by the brothers. They hate Joseph and devise a simple plan to murder him. Like all simple plans, it soon gets complicated. Big brother Reuben says, "Wait up, let's not kill him." Plan A becomes Plan B. The brothers decide to throw Joseph into a pit and let him die there. Reuben figures he can come back when no one is watching and rescue his brother.

It's demanding work removing someone's fancy clothes and tossing him into a pit, so afterwards the brothers take a break for lunch. While they are chewing their food, a caravan of Ishmaelites passes by. Plan B becomes plan C. Brother Judah says, "Let's make some money here and sell little bro to the Ishmaelites". Problem is, some Midianite traders get to the pit first, pull Joseph up and sell him to the Ishmaelites for 20 pieces of silver.

Reuben is first to arrive at the empty pit and he thinks Joseph is dead. The brothers act quickly; they take Joseph's long-sleeved coat, splash it with goat's blood and bring it to their father. Seeing the bloodied coat, Jacob assumes his favorite son is dead.

In Egypt, Joseph is bought by a certain Mr. Potiphar, who is like the head of Egypt's central intelligence agency. The story says Joseph has a run-in with Mrs. Potiphar. She likes him but he does not want to play (Genesis 39:7); it's a case of sexual harassment in the workplace and Joseph runs leaving his robe behind. Mrs. Potiphar accuses Joseph of attempted rape and presses charges. Poor innocent Joseph is thrown in prison. He is about 17 at the time.

It is while in prison that the dreamer Joseph becomes an interpreter of dreams. When Pharaoh has a couple of troubling dreams about cows eating cows and grain swallowing grain, Joseph is rushed from the dungeon to interpret. He does such a good job that he is promoted to Pharaoh's right-hand man. Pharaoh gives Joseph his signet ring and dresses him in garments of fine linen and puts a gold chain around his neck (Genesis 41:42). Joseph is made into an honorary Egyptian, given an Egyptian name that is complicated and hyphenated and begins with a Z. He marries an Egyptian woman, Asenath, and they have two kids.

Seven years later, there is a world famine and Joseph's brothers come to Egypt to buy food. Guess who is in charge of selling food?

None other than Jospeph. Nearly 20 years had passed and the brothers do not recognize him. How could they? He now has an Egyptian name, an Egyptian wife, Egyptian children, an Egyptian job, and for all purposes, the man walks like an Egyptian! But Joseph, he recognizes his brothers.

Joseph, we are told, did not immediately reveal his identity to his brothers. He allows them to mistake him for nothing but an ordinary Egyptian, a bureaucrat in charge of the food-sales department. But there came a time, we are told, when Joseph could no longer contain himself and he broke down and wept. His weeping was so loud that the Egyptians heard him. He wept so hard the household of Pharaoh heard him. And then he looked at his brothers and spoke to them and said, "Come closer! I am Joseph. I am Joseph, your brother."

The Joseph story has so many facets and angles depending on where you are standing when the light strikes this diamond of an account. Using the Joseph story, we can preach a sermon on forgiveness. Joseph is the example par excellence of forgiveness. He forgives his brothers who had attempted to murder him and then sold him into slavery. Even in the final episode when the brothers are afraid saying, "What if Joseph still bears a grudge against us and pays us back in full for all the wrong that we did to him?", Joseph tells them, "Fear not! Even though you intended to do harm to me, God intended it for good." And we are told he reassured them, speaking kindly to them (Genesis 50:15-21).

Surely then, the Joseph story is about forgiveness. The story makes the important point that anything and everything is forgivable.

For some of us, the light can strike the Joseph story in another way. We might point out that the Joseph story is not about Joseph but about God. It is a story of a life-giving God whose extravagant love cannot be stopped by the desert, by misfortune, by slavery. A God who brings life to places of barrenness and emptiness. Listen up! The desert cannot stop God! We are talking about a God who makes Sarah burst into laughter with the promise of a child in her old age. We are talking about a God who opens the wombs of Leah, Rebekah and Rachel and blesses them with children. We are talking about a God who blesses Joseph in the land of his misfortune. This is a God who, when Jospeh's situation seems hopeless, gives him a powerful position, a loving wife and two beautiful sons. And, overwhelmed by God's goodness, Joseph names his one son "God has helped me forget my hardship" and the other son "God has made me fruitful in a desert."

So the Joseph story is really a testimony about God, who does not wait for conditions to be right in order to act; God acts even under the most hostile and seemingly impossible circumstances.

This is a story about forgiveness. Yes! This is a story about God. Yes! Stand somewhere else and this Joseph story is a warning about the perils of assuming privilege over others, of believing that we have more rights than the rest of God's children.

Joseph's story, like each of our lifestories, reaches way back. In Joseph's case, it stretches back to great-grandpa Abram and great-grandma Sarai. You remember Abram and Sarai, that old couple traveling light and running on nearly empty. They are old and childless with only a promise in their luggage. In Genesis chapter 12, the Lord said to Abram, "Go from your country and your kindred and your father's house to the land that I will show you. I will make you a great nation, and I will bless you, and make your name great, so that you will be a blessing. I will bless those who bless you, and the one who curse you I will curse; and in you all the families of the earth shall be blessed."

They travel on the promise of becoming privileged, part of God's favorite family. Joseph's great-grandparents Abram and Sarai wanted to be the best, the biggest, the most godly, the most famous family on earth. They were promised to be the privileged ones, with advantages and special rights. And after God had changed their names to Abraham and Sarah, the son Isaac is born to them, and the story privileges Isaac as if he is Abraham's only son. But wait, Isaac might be Abraham's most beloved son, but he is certainly not his only son.

Sarai's African maid Hagar had been used as a surrogate mother when Sarai momentarily had a panic attack, doubted God's promise and faith-faint Sarai, thinking she was too old to conceive, helped God by giving Abram the slave-woman Hagar, who bore Abram his first son Ishmael. And what goes around comes around. Two generations later, the Ishmaelites buy Joseph as a slave and take him to Egypt. God uses the Ishmaelites to rescue Joseph from the threat of death at the hands of his brothers.

But back to Abram and Sarai. In spite of Sarai's panic and anxiety, God made good God's word because God always does. In her old age, Sarah conceived and gave birth to Isaac, which was Sarah's first child and Abraham's second. With Isaac's arrival, Hagar and Ishmael are no longer needed. They are violently thrown out of the story like desert trash. It is violent because maintaining privilege so often requires violence. People are used as stepping stones, discarded as soon as they are not required by the storyline. Family secrets. Family skeletons. Family scandals. Once they distrusted God, Abraham and Sarah's family got caught in a vicious cycle, which continued the theme of privileging one over the other. Jacob is favored over Esau; Rachel is favored over Leah; Joseph is favored over all the rest.

The simple story of Joseph is loaded, a landmine. And the problem lies in the nature of stories. Stories work through both the spoken and the unspoken, the layers beneath the surface. Much is left out. For the story to work, the narrator must do violence to history. In order for there to be a coherent narrative with a plot that develops from a beginning, to a middle and end, we are obliged to order and rank events, edit them, place value on certain persons and say nothing about other characters.

In order for a story to work, even the story of our lives, certain people and certain events have to be assigned to the margins so that other events and other persons can be made central. Indeed, the craft of storytelling is one of knowing what and how to privilege some events and persons over others and how to influence, cajole, and even threaten the audience into accepting the choices and collaborate with the story.

Like all of life, it is a matter of making choices, deciding what should be reported and what should not. Who should be mentioned, who should not. In order to say something about anything, we have to be silent about some things.

Family stories work in the same way. They seem programmed to remember certain incidents and forget others. The worldview held by families is not easily reprogrammed. Old traditions die hard, if they die at all. These are habits of the heart founded in a narrative theology deeply steeped in a God who privileges some over others, giving Abraham's nation special rights, a God who celebrates Isaac's birthday and ignores Ishmael's existence.

With such a theological framework, no wonder Abraham's descendants operate by preferencing and privileging and ranking people. Joseph is born into that kind of family. He is first child to his mother Rachel, and although Joseph is not his father's first or only son, his father treats him as though he is the first and only. His father Jacob makes him a coat with long sleeves, which is an extravagance and waste of fabric in a large family of five wives and 12 sons and unnumbered daughters. In today's world, Jacob's large family would shop at Thrifty, apart from Joseph that is, who would use daddy's credit card in the town's most expensive boutiques. Jacob's large family would wear homespun clothes, while Joseph would dazzle in the world's first designer garment, a technicolor coat with a gold "Joe" for a logo. With such pampering, such special treatment, such favoritism, no wonder Joseph dreams of being a prince, a king, a ruler.

Joseph dreams that all his brothers are his humble subjects who bow down before him, which should not surprise us. I have gone to schools and universities alongside many privileged kids and know that privileged kids are able to dream of being a secretary of state, chairwoman of the board, manager of the department, top of their profession; they walk and act and speak as though everybody else is supposed to serve and follow them, as though the path to success is carved out in advance. So now you see why Joseph's brothers got fed up and planned to get rid of him.

To understand the story for our time, you don't need a commentary. To borrow from Karl Barth, you should read the Bible in one hand and the newspaper in the other. As an example, we can take a Dateline report on Rwanda, in which the reporter compared the international community's assistance to Kosovo with its seeming indifference to Rwanda.

I watched with tears running down my face as the report showed scenes of Rwandans drinking water contaminated by dead bodies. There were pictures of a 14-year-old Rwandan child whose parents, aunts and uncles were murdered and who is now father and mother to a family of six. These scenes were contrasted with those from Kosovo showing children airlifted to the United States and offered American citizenship. During the Kosovo crisis the news seemed to be updated minute by minute. But the 800,000 Rwandans who were chopped up like firewood received scant coverage.

Why this difference in priorities? Why favor some and ignore others? Some say it's racism. Some say it's compassion fatigue. Some pundits argue the "Black Hawk Down" disaster in Somalia deterred the international community from further involvement in Africa. Perhaps, and it hurts me to say so, it is a question of ranking people by geographical location. It seems absurd, but could it be that Kosovo is considered more important and pressing than Rwanda? Could it be that Kosovo belongs to the industrialized world whereas Rwanda is faraway in "darkest Africa"? We know, thank goodness, that genocide and ethnic cleansing are no longer tolerated on Western soil, and should the killing start, help is promised in a handshake. But in Africa, the violence is often allowed to spiral out of control without the international community bothering to intervene. And when help comes, it is often too little, too late.

We read the papers and like Joseph, all we can do is weep. We weep so loudly and so deeply that the whole world hears, breaking the silence, not caring if the Egyptians and the house of Pharaoh hear us!

One poet helps us when he writes:

"Crying out loud and weeping are great resources.
A nursing mother, all she does
is wait to hear her child.
Just a beginning-whimper,
and she's there.
God created the child that is your wanting,
so that it might cry out, so that milk might come.
Cry out! Don't be stolid and silent with your pain.
Lament! And let the milk of loving flow into you
Give your weakness to One who helps"

Joseph is no longer impassive and silent. He weeps and the pain gushes out of him hard and loud. And then a strange thing happens. After the weeping, the story shifts. When Joseph meets his brothers, it seems that exile and slavery have changed him. He has learned that relationship as a brother is to be valued over privilege, ruthless careerism and the hunger for power. He no longer dreams of being the king to whom his brothers bow down as they now do in Egypt. Joseph has come to his senses and recognizes that to be a brother is of utmost value.

When he meets his brothers, Joseph weeps and calls them to come closer. And he tells them, "I am Joseph. I am your brother!"

He claims his relationship to them as their brother. Did you hear that? Joseph does not identify himself as his father's privileged or preferred son. He names himself: I am Joseph. And he identifies himself with the most powerful relationship of all: I am your brother. Come closer, he tells them. Come, let us close the distance between us. The physical distance. Come closer, let us bridge the gap between us. Come closer. I am your brother.

This story makes me want to cry out saying, "I am Joseph, I am your brother!" You see, I am not "the black woman, the African pastor". I am Mukokinyitte, Grace, your sister. I have a name and you and I are in the kind of relationship that even betrayal cannot erase. I am Joseph, I am your brother. I am Grace. I am your sister.

8

Fire in My Bones

The word that came to Jeremiah from the Lord: "Come, go down to the potter's house, and there I will let you hear my words." So I went down to the potter's house, and there he was working at his wheel. The vessel he was making of clay was spoiled in the potter's hand, and he reworked it into another vessel, as seemed good to him. (Jeremiah 18: 1-4)

Once in a while, God resorts to drama in order to catch our attention, in order to get through to us in the hustle and bustle and fogginess of our lives. One of the most dramatic lives in the Bible is that of the prophet Jeremiah. Time and time again, God asks Jeremiah to choose theatrical gestures and images and mimicry and pantomime in order to communicate God's message. Jeremiah is the visual-aids prophet, the prophet who fascinates us with drama. He is the one who stirs us, who goes to the heart of each question and disturbs us by telling it as it is.

Jeremiah is too dramatic for some, too serious for others. Some might even say he's too unstable. Most of all, Jeremiah is remembered as the weeping prophet because as you move from chapter and verse to chapter and verse over and over again, Jeremiah weeps for God's people.

We are introduced to Jeremiah when the word of God comes to him and it comes in the same way it comes to us because God is often the one who takes the initiative, who asks where we are. God's word comes and the word is clear that you are God's idea. You are God's property.

God's word comes to Jeremiah in chapter 1:4: "Before I formed you in your mother's womb, I knew you. Before you were born I called you to be a prophet to the nations." I knew you, I formed you, I consecrated you, I appointed you. Before you were a bleep on the radar, before you were a twinkle in anybody's eye, before you were a picture on the ultrasound, God knew you and consecrated you. Thus Augustine of Hippo writes, "You have made us for thyself O Lord and our hearts are restless until they find rest in thee".

Jeremiah's first response to God is one we have seen over and over again. He says, "I don't want to be a prophet". Thank you God, but no thanks. Jeremiah knows that there is nothing good that comes to a prophet. A prophet's life is hard, a life of constant rejection. And so Jeremiah says, "No thanks, Lord. I am only a boy. I am too young, too inadequate, too inexperienced. I cannot even speak. I have plenty of excuses as to why I am the wrong candidate".

God replies, "Don't say you are too young. What has age got to do with being called to serve me?" God tells Jeremiah, "I will give you my words" and God touches Jeremiah's lips and gives him the words. And so Jeremiah goes out as a fired-up prophet. He asks the people to repent but the people say, "We don't want to hear it and we don't plan on obeying it."

And so the drama begins. Gods begins to reach the hard-heartedness of the people by using visual aids so they will remember God's message. God tells Jeremiah, "Go buy a linen loincloth". In chapter 13, Jeremiah buys a loincloth and for us today that's like buying a pair of boxer shorts. "Go buy the best silk boxer shorts you can afford and wear them". So Jeremiah goes shopping and he comes back with boxer shorts. God asks,

"How do they feel?" Jeremiah says, "Good".

And God says, "Take them off and go to the river Euphrates and there find a cleft in the rock, somewhere wet, and bury the boxer shorts". And Jeremiah does that and then a few months go by and God says to Jeremiah, "Go dig up the boxer shorts," and he does that. And, as we can imagine, the shorts are ruined. They have holes in them, they are full of creepy crawlies. And God tells Jeremiah, "Put them on". And Jeremiah says what you and I would say: "No way!".

And God says, "Exactly, that's the point". Being in relationship with a sinful people is like being asked to wear boxer shorts full of creepy crawlies. We ask God to be in relationship with us, constantly coming before God and yet we refuse to repent of our sins, to turn around. And still God asks for an intimate relationship with us, which is like asking God to put on those long-buried, vermin-infested boxer shorts. So Jeremiah goes and tells the people, "Repent, God has made you for relationship, made you to be fine and intimate in relationship with God, that is what you were created and formed for".

And still the people do not listen, so in chapter 18 God tells Jeremiah, "Go to the potter's house and I am going to teach you a lesson there". And Jeremiah goes to the potter's house and he watches the potter make a clay jar. The potter is working hard at the wheel, fashioning a clay pot. But as Jeremiah watches, the clay goes bad. The potter removes the bad clay and begins to refashion the clay pot into something smaller. And God tells Jeremiah, "Enough. Tell my people that nothing you have done is so bad that God cannot remove the bad clay and make something of you. Yes, perhaps a lesser vessel but God can still make something out of your life."

All that is required is repentance, a turnaround, a change of heart. God can make something out of you. No clay can ever be written off in the hands of the potter. That's why Jeremiah goes to the people and says, "All that God requires of you is repentance. God can refashion us. God can make something out of us no matter what has gone wrong with us. God can make something of our lives".

The people still do not want to hear it. They don't want to obey. They don't buy the clay story. And so God tells Jeremiah, "I want you to go to the market and buy a clay pot" and Jeremiah does that. God tells him, "Gather all the elders, people and priests. Gather them around and tell them, as you raise the clay pot high, 'Don't you realize, no matter how high you fly, you are still the clay pot in God's hands. Don't you realize you are a clay pot in God's hands and God raises you up high. And sometimes in our success and good health, we are still the clay pot in God's hands' ". And God tells Jeremiah, "Then once you have said this, I want you to raise the clay pot high and ask, 'What would happen if the potter let go of the clay pot?' "

Jeremiah lifts the pot high and lets go and things turn bad for Israel. And as the Israelites are led into exile, Jeremiah weeps out the book of Lamentation. But for us the story does not stop there because God is incredible, expanding the options over and over again. In the story of Jesus, Christ is God saying, "I love you too much to simply drop you and let you smash".

Time and time again, God urges us to choose a better life for ourselves, our community and our world. Choose life. Nothing is ever so bad that God cannot remake it, even if it means making a lesser vessel. Choose life. For God so loved the world, that whoever believes in God's son will not perish but have everlasting life.

9

"Mom, Fix It!"

But a Samaritan while traveling came near him; and when he saw him, he was moved with pity. He went to him and bandaged his wounds, having poured oil and wine on them. Then he put him on his own animal, brought him to an inn, and took care of him. (Luke 10:33-34)

Today I was listening once again to Jesus telling the "Parable of the Good Samaritan", and as I did so I began thinking of the often unrecognized work that mothers do of fixing broken things. Moms play a vital role in keeping things from getting broken and when things break or are damaged or injured, it is mom's job to fix them. Moms are supposed to keep and make things right while armed with nothing more than a paper clip, a kiss or simple words. They are supposed to be able to weave a story out of thin air, and moms are expected to compose songs complete with music and lyrics that make the monsters disappear and the world a safe place again.

Moms have learnt how to fix not just broken chains in commodes or bicycles that won't peddle, they also fix trains, trucks and tanks. To be a mom is to be a fixer and mender and repairer and restorer and peacemaker and peacekeeper and a visionary leader. I know this to be true now that I am the mom of a 2-year-old boy. I spend significant amounts of time each day making sure things don't break and when something breaks or stops working, I am called upon to "Fix it!"

I was thinking about the role of moms fixing things while listening to Jesus telling the story of the Good Samaritan. A traveler is robbed on the road from the city of Jerusalem to the town of Jericho. And on that windy and steep road, the robbers did more than steal the traveler's wallet, watch, class ring and donkey: they humiliated him. They stripped the man naked, taking his cloak, his shorts, his socks and boots. Furthermore, the thugs, their cruelty knowing no end, beat up the traveler. I imagine they slapped him and punched him and kicked him. And brutal as they were, they did not kill their victim, relieving him of his poor, humiliated and excruciating condition. No sir! They left him in the scorching sun with his life hanging on a thread. Robbed, stripped and bloodied, the traveler was left to die alone.

I count myself with Mother Teresa of Calcutta, who once explained and justified her work by saying, "No one, however sick, however repulsive, should have to die alone." That traveler on the road from Jerusalem to Jericho was robbed, beaten and left to die alone. If I had been traveling on that same road with my son, there is no doubt that he would have pointed to the man in the ditch, looked at me and demanded, "Mom, fix it!"

In retelling the story of the robbery, I have concentrated on the intense violence of the attack. But Jesus recounts the events with quick, detached precision, so that it is easy to miss the viciousness. In wondering why Jesus did not linger on the graphic details, I find myself inventing a thousand alternative explanations. Perhaps Jesus' audience had personal knowledge of attacks and robberies and so there was no need to be explicit. As a scholar, I know that Jesus and his audience lived in a world full of physical violence, in which hunger, poverty, robbery and general insecurity were commonplace.

In quite a few of the stories Jesus told, we get a firsthand look at the violence of first-century Palestine. Do you remember the story in Luke 12 of the houseowner who is ready day and night, guarding against a thief? And there is the story of a slave who, when promoted, beats the heck out of the other slaves, women included, causing his master to punish him with a thorough thrashing, even chopping him to bits (Luke 12:45-48)? Remember the king's birthday that turned into a halloween of sorts when the king loses his head, chops off the prophet's head and serves it to his daughter on a silver platter (Mark 6:21-28)?

What's more, there are some scholars who point out that it is no coincidence that the first folks to hear "Peace on Earth" that first Christmas night were shepherds. In rural antiquity, shepherds knew all about violence; they often caused it themselves by keeping flocks belonging to others and turning a blind eye when their flocks trampled over the cultivated fields of settled communities.

Let's face it, Jesus, the prince of peace, did not live in a bubble in some fantasy, never-never land. Jesus lived in a world complicated by violence; it was as insecure as we know our own world to be. So, most likely, when his audience heard of the violent robbery on the Jerusalem to Jericho road, they said, "Yep. Happens all the time."

If you are hearing this story for the first time, let me mention that the robbers are mentioned only once (Luke 10:30); they get half a line of text and then nothing more is said about them. Don't expect vivid descriptions of how the thugs are sought out, hunted down and brought to justice. Don't expect to read anything about the robbers ending up in some hot eternity in the abyss where they become meat for hell's grill.

I don't know about you, but I have struggled with the story at this point. I have often asked Jesus to pause and explain the thugs. I have often spoken to Jesus about my disappointment at this loose end. My response is no doubt influenced by a storytelling tradition which always brings the bad guys to justice. I have a problem with thugs and murderers dying a natural death in their old age. I want them to be punished for their crimes and the good guy to get the loot and ride off into the sunset. But Jesus does not tell that kind of story.

While I long to hear about the thugs being chased across the desert and brought to justice, Jesus moves along quickly with the story. This bothered me until I heard the children's entertainer Fred Rogers advising adults how to speak to children about violent stories on the news. Fred Rogers tells us about his own childhood. When he saw scary things on the news, his mother would say to him, "Look for the helpers. You will always find people who are helping."

According to the parable, the priest and Levite saw the wounded man and passed on the other side of the path. Without hesitation, commentators and interpreters of this text have reprimanded and poured scorn on the priest and the Levite. At times these commentators seem to go too far. They make it look as though all priests and Levites are callous and merciless. In fact, such an interpretation spills over and makes the religion of the priests and Levites look faulty and suspicious. Next thing, unsuspectingly, the seeds of anti-Semitism start germinating in our reading and interpretations.

So let me say right off: there is nothing wrong with priests and Levites. Some of the Gospel's best friends are priests. Think about it. One of the first important characters we meet in Luke's Gospel is a priest named Zechariah. His wife is Betsy. Zechariah is described as righteous, living blamelessly. He is juxtaposed against the wicked King Herod when Luke says, "In the days of King Herod of Judea, there was a priest named Zechariah" (Luke 1:5). So you see, priests are not bad at all.

Think about it: John the Baptist's father was a priest. Similarly, if you had asked anybody in the early church, they would have told you that some of their finest members were Levites. Think of Barnabas, who Luke tells us "was a Levite" and he was generous and such a source of encouragement for the little fledgling church in Jerusalem they nicknamed him "son of encouragement". That Levite sold his land and put every single cent in the offertory basket (Acts 4:36).

Because I know some good priests and good Levites, I want to give the priest and Levite who passed the beat-up traveler the benefit of the doubt. I know that someone somewhere will look at job descriptions and go on and on about cultic and ritual purity and the consequences of holy people touching corpses. But I will nip that one in the bud: the need for compassion overrides cultural, cultic, religious or imaginary fears of impurity. And still I give the priest and Levite the benefit of the doubt because I imagine that they passed by simply because they could not "fix it". I want to imagine they were overwhelmed. These are temple workers, not doctors or paramedics. They don't have the know-how to fix it; don't have the tools to fix it; don't have the ingenuity that Moms seem to have when called upon to fix things with calming words or their bare hands.

If we are going to reprimand and scorn the priest and Levite, no one gets off the hook. We must use the same standard for anyone who passes by without stopping to help. We would have to reprimand ourselves as the church. Too often we have passed by on the other side of those who are broken and injured and humiliated on life's road. We can try to let ourselves off the hook by claiming we are overwhelmed by the huge size of global problems. The mountain of awful statistics seems insurmountable. Think of the millions of children under the age of five dying every year from hunger and malnutrition. That is so overwhelming, it can numb us into inertia!

We might try to hide behind the fact that we are ill-equipped or inadequately trained or financed. Many of us would be willing to drop what we are doing today and help. But what can one person, one congregation, one mission trip do to dent the size and scale of the AIDS pandemic? By 2010, according to the United Nations, there will be 107 million orphans in the world. Of those, 25 million or nearly a quarter will be AIDS orphans. Fourteen million children have lost one or both parents to AIDS. This is too much for one person or one congregation or one community or one country to comprehend, let alone solve.

I am not throwing any stones here, not apportioning blame, because I have sometimes been as guilty as the priest or Levite. I have sometimes passed by a problem crying out to be solved. But lately, in the face of any crisis, just when I am about to cross the road and pass on by, my child's confident voice stops me dead in my tracks and says, "Mom, fix it!" It can be disturbing listening to Jesus with one ear and listening to my child with the other. I listen to Jesus, who does not dwell on describing violence and instead focuses on the helper. He takes less than one line to tell of the thugs' terror and violence but devotes three whole verses to the Samaritan. That's a lot of words, a lot of ink. When I am in mom-mode, the Samaritan reminds me of a mother figure. He uses whatever he has; he is a merchant who does not carry bottles of water, so he bathes the traveler's wounds with oil and wine. He is like a mother using her ingenuity in a crisis. See! The Samaritan tears his own garments to use as bandages. And like a mother, he stays by the stranger's bedside the whole night, wiping the man's fevered brow with a cold cloth. The Samaritan is driven not by expertise but by compassion. It is the same gut-feeling of mercy which propels mothers to operate outside their common sense, taking risks and daring to help.

What do I have to give my child as I hold my Bible in one hand and the newspaper in the other? I want to teach him how to see the people who are helping. And I want to teach him to see them not just during times of war and conflict, but during times of peace. I want him to learn how to see the people who not only fix things but who keep things from getting broken. If during peaceful periods my child should ever be asked if he fears the threat of a nuclear bomb or world war, I want him to be like the child who answered saying, "No, I am not afraid. My mom works hard every day to make sure it does not happen."

"Mom, fix it!" In the face of tragedy, there is great hope for our world because I can see those who are helping. Keep your eyes peeled for those who are helping; in season and out of season. And perhaps you too will decide to be a helper and "to cast [your] lot with those who age after age, perversely, with no extraordinary power, reconstitute the world." Amen.

10

Islands and Visions

After this I looked, and there was a great multitude that no one could count, from every nation, from all tribes and peoples and languages, standing before the throne and before the Lamb, robed in white, with palm branches in their hands. They cried out in a loud voice saying, "Salvation belongs to our God who is seated on the throne, and to the Lamb!" (Revelation 7:9-10)

Behold, a vision! Visions are vintage Revelation. In one of John's visions, he saw so many people, it was impossible to count them. Tons and tons of people. Loads and loads of them. A multitude. Not just the 144,000 good people we have heard rumors about, but people from every nation were there. Every tribe was there. Every race was there. Every language was there. What John means to say is that the whole world was there. Dressed in white robes and waving palm branches. What a sight! Spectacular? Yes. Mindboggling? Yes. Possible? No! No! No!

Some might even say this vision is unachievable. We know too much; too much water has flowed under the bridge. This is one of those visions that are shelved in the reference section under Y as in "Yeah, right, dream on". Am I pessimistic? Not really. Just painfully realistic about who we have been in our past, who we are today and who I fear we will continue to be.

It is almost as though human nature is programmed with a chip that makes us wacko about winning regardless of those we hurt or humiliate. In any group or mob, there are many who are desperately eager for their view to win at all costs. In religious matters, we want our denomination to win as the most Christian. We want our culture to triumph as the most authentic, our nation to be the most powerful, our economy to be the most dominant, and our tribe the most indigenous.

Let's face it, let's be brave about it and admit the truth. Time and time again in the history of human beings, we have been unable to live with anyone different from us. Our history shows that when we have encountered others who are different from us, we have tried to silence them. We have silenced through ridicule, through stereotyping, and through humiliation. We have silenced by killing people who are different from ourselves.

So much of human history is about conquering and domination and slavery and imperialism and colonialism and exploitation and racism and tribalism and sexism and bloodshed and genocide and holocausts and ethnic cleansing. Our track record in relationships with different people is so bad that I am not optimistic it can be salvaged by visions that dress up everybody in white robes, place them in a choir and give them a bunch of palm branches to wave.

It is not surprising that we are constantly bombarded with story after story of how impossible it is for different people to gather in the same place without somebody silencing somebody else. Every day, the news channels carry stories of people gunning each other down because they are Roman Catholic in Protestant zones, Kikuyus in Pokot land of Kenya, or Palestinians in…is it occupied or unoccupied territories?

Every day, newspapers are full of stories of policies voted in and laws passed to keep some people living the same old ghetto lives because they are black or colored or boat people in countries that are suspicious of diversity. We have seen documentaries about people who, with the help of clergy, chopped each other up because one group's noses were different from the other group's, because one group's customs were different from the other's.

Not even the supposedly objective, fair and impartial world of sports is untouched by the need to win over others at all costs. Let me tell you about Kenyans. We Kenyans have a thing about winning long distance races. We assume that when it comes to marathons and half-marathons, Kenyans will always win. We have almost come to consider it our birthright. Even without the million-dollar training and without being brought up using super hi-tech Nike running shoes and without the hiphugging, aerodynamic designer tracksuits, Kenyan runners win races. A cause for celebration? You would think so, but not everyone is happy when Africans win every long distance race.

It turns out that people get threatened, or at best bored and indifferent, when folks from other nations and other tribes look like they are taking over and will win every time. Things got so messy in 1997 that the organizers of the Bolder Boulder 10-km elite race in Colorado ruled that Americans were to be allowed unlimited participants while other countries were limited to only three runners. Bolder Boulder's organizers were frustrated by foreign dominance in the race: the top ten finishers in 1997 were all foreign, and eight of them were Kenyan.

We do not need to go so far as some and accuse the organizers of racism. We can call them insensitive and unfair. The organizers crassly admitted, "American sponsors want American winners" and to help them along it was decided that any American who finished in the top five would receive double the prize money awarded to a foreign runner.

Thank goodness that this backfired and common sense prevailed. After furious protests from foreigners and Americans alike, the organizers again changed the rules, deciding that each national team in the elite race, including the American team, was to be limited to three runners. We will never again see Kenyans taking eight of the top ten places but nor will be see national pride taking precedence over sportsmanship.

Human beings are irredeemably sensitive about who wins. People are sensitive about differences. We are nervous around people who are different from us. We get so nervous that we build walls to keep them out. We get sensitive about the idea of different languages. Something about foreigners makes us anxious. Instead of embracing or understanding difference, we mock it. When we cannot understand or be understood, we fear that we will not be able and allowed to participate. No wonder differences make us nervous!

Being different in our world is risky. If you want to be different in our world get ready to be excluded, misunderstood and constantly under suspicion. Being different in our world can get you killed. If you dare to be different, be prepared to die. That's why, according to my reading of our bloody human history and paranoid human nature, John's vision in Revelation 7 is moot. It is impossible because we cannot erase the memory of the injury we have caused each other in the past. OK, maybe we might go so far as to forgive each other but I doubt we will be crazy enough to forget the harm we have caused each other repeatedly, severely, deeply. I doubt we will ever be crazy enough to dare to trust each other after what we have been through.

Waving palm branches is not good enough. So what is the alternative? If were to give advice, I might cynically say we should look to those among us who are smart enough to know how to blend in, toe the line, lose the accent, pretend to be what they are not. It's not that difficult. With resolve and a stiff upper lip, it is possible to fake that you are one of the gang.

Knowing what we know, it is no wonder we don't read Revelation anymore. The whole book of Revelation seems like a mistake. Consider the bizarre, psychedelic images. There is no way the writer could have been stable, credible or in touch with reality. Let's not beat about the bush; he was seeing way beyond the horizon I am seeing.

The context of Revelation is islands and we should not expect otherwise. The writer, he calls himself John, was stuck on an island called Patmos when he wrote the book. Patmos is out there in the sea somewhere near mainland Greece. These days, Patmos is a tourist hotspot full of Bible pilgrims who want to see where John was living when he saw what he was seeing. Because of all that pilgrim traffic, Patmos has been dubbed the Jerusalem of the Aegean Sea.

But when John wrote Revelation, Patmos was a hotspot of an entirely different sort. Delete pilgrims and insert convicts. In addition, Patmos was one big rock of an island where not much grew there. Not coffee, not potatoes, not even weeds. Nothing grew there that could be eaten, drunk or smoked. Nobody went there unless they were sent. It was like death row.

What was John doing on this godforsaken island? Was he a criminal? In some ways he was because he had been sent there against his will by the authorities. As he put it, he was on Patmos "because of the word of God and the testimony of Jesus." He claims he was banished by the political authorities of his time because of his faith and his preaching. Religious persecution in other words. Today, John might be considered a dissident, a political prisoner.

But, let's not go too fast. Some scholars doubt that John was a religious prisoner. Some say there were the usual repressions here and there during the time John's letter was written, but his claims of persecution are exaggerated. Other scholars say that John's claim of banishment is possible because banishment was a common punishment during the imperial period. The empire got rid of political agitators by isolating them so they would not influence society. In other words, some scholars say John was indeed a political prisoner.

As usual, scholars never agree about anything. But that's all right because if nothing else, scholars always help us remember that no matter how thin you cut it, there are always two sides to any issue, and sometimes there are three, four or more. So to keep a balance, let us say that whatever the historical facts, John believed he was persecuted for his faith. And he believed he was stuck on Patmos because his faith gave him the kind of visions that made political authorities nervous.

His faith and visions made governments uneasy. His faith gave him the kind of visions that saw the world afresh and anew and recreated, full of possibilities that many had come to believe were impossible. John's visions transcended the desolate world of history and dared to believe that our future together is not written by our past with each other. John's visions threatened the existing order and those who controlled it. So they packed him off to Patmos. Being sent to Patmos was like putting a hole in the bucket called life. Your life was wasted there. But not quite; prison and exile cannot put a stop to visions of a better future. Not even the most powerful repressive systems can stop people from dreaming and imagining and desiring a better life for all.

Nelson Mandela was banished by a white, racist government to Robben Island for 27 long years. Mandela went to prison as a father of six young children and came out as a grandfather to 21 grandchildren and as great-grandfather to three great-grandchildren. In 27 years on godforsaken Robben Island, he had missed marriages, births, naming ceremonies and funerals.

What got him there in the first place was a vision that made him a very dangerous man. Mandela was born and grew up in apartheid, a system which used the full force of law to keep races apart. Blacks and whites could not travel on the same buses, use the same water fountains, or sit on the same benches. If you broke the rules, you were arrested, fined, beaten, tortured. Being born into that system, the safest thing to do if you didn't want trouble was to make do by the system and carry on somehow.

If Mandela had done that, he would not have ended up on Robben Island. It might have been possible for him to have hated white people and at the same time have avoided them and trouble by staying in the homelands assigned to black South Africans. Or perhaps he could have fled the country, as many did, and moved to Sweden or Norway or the United States. If he had, he would not have ended up on Robben Island. But Mandela had a vision which dismissed apartheid, which dismissed the history apartheid had painted. Mandela saw the future and he dared to dream that it would be brighter and fairer. Mandela made apartheid lawmakers nervous in 1962 when he said: "I detest racialism because

I regard it as a barbaric thing, whether it comes from a white man or whether it comes from a black man".

In the infamous Rivornia trial in 1962, Mandela said: "I have fought against white domination, and I have fought against black domination. I have cherished the ideal of a democratic and free society in which all persons live together in harmony and with equal opportunities. It is an ideal which I hope to live for and to achieve. But if needs be, it is an ideal for which I am prepared to die."

Achievable harmony. Achievable justice. Achievable fairness. And achieving these fine things is worth dying for. Such thinking is seditious, subversive and dangerous.

My favorite writer these days is a Bengali woman who lives on an island, the island of Manhattan. Her name is Gayatri Chakravorty Spivak. In her work she talks about the importance of being in relationships with people who are different from us. She says it is critical to be in relationships with people who are different from us because the social positions we occupy make certain knowledge impossible to access. That kind of knowledge is not the same as information you can acquire from a book, or by downloading a program or by living in a certain place. Spivak says there is a kind of knowledge that comes only by being in relationship with someone different from us. The kind of relationship she is talking about is not simply a case of being friendly but learning to speak to that other person in such a way that they take us seriously. Spivak says the relationship can be considered successful only if the other person is able to answer back.

How do you do that? What is the secret? How do you get into such relationships? Spivak talks about unlearning privilege. When we no longer consciously or unconsciously assume we have some rights that another person does not have.

Unlearning privilege is not automatic. Privilege is often already written into the system. Privileging some over others is what keeps things running smoothly. Unlearning privilege means shifting from self-preoccupation into looking at how those who are different from us are being treated.

Let me break it down and deal with my social location as a Meru woman. Unlearning privilege in my tribe, the Meru, revolves around the issue of gender. If Meru men unlearn privilege then even the kind of food people are served will change. In Meru when there is a feast at a wedding, funeral or ceremony of some sort, we often slaughter a cow, and there is a code for which parts of the animal different genders and different age groups eat.

Throughout Meru history, women eat the intestines. In America these are called chitlings. We call them matumbo. Over the years, Meru women have learned to fix matumbo to make it very tasty, and I like them, especially the furry kind. In Meru, a man would rather starve than eat women's food.

When I was home two summers ago, I preached a sermon in my home church, Mwanika Methodist Church, and said: "The good news Jesus brings to the Meru people is that Meru women can know without doubt that we too are beloved children of God and we do not have to eat only intestines; we can eat whatever piece of meat we want." You should have seen the surprise. People were shocked to hear of such a Gospel. It was scandalous. A few women, including my mother, clapped. Some people laughed thinking it was a big joke. They tried to imagine a woman eating ribs or sirloin steak; what a ridiculous image, women eating men's food and acting like pseudo-males. Most of the people said that too much education had ruined me and caused my outrageous remarks.

John saw what will happen to us and it is good. John saw our achievable future together and it is something we must work toward. According to John, our future is not about conquering our past, or reversing our history, or erasing our traditions and languages. John saw us living together and making it through our differences. Making it through like the Lamb who will be our host.

Can you see John's vision? Can you see us daring to live with each other in radical ways that overcome the ghosts of our past? Can you see it yet? Can you see us stirring up the system by daring to believe in subversive ideals of justice and mercy and God for all? Have you seen the vision that makes the hardships and loneliness and sadness and struggles and often pointless existence of islands and isolation bearable?

Alison Head from that island called England has re-written John's vision in these words:

Then I saw the earth blazing with sunlight:
I saw children laughing as they learned the secrets of the earth
From people who smiled and shared their knowledge.
I saw the world celebrating carnival: black and white,
Protestant and Catholic, Christians and Jews,
All joining hands and dancing through the countryside
And the city streets.

I saw the streets a mass of color
Where people left their jobs and houses to join the fun:
And then I saw people returning to jobs
Where they felt the fulfillment of creation.

I saw faces full of peace and joy,
I saw children full of food and excitement;
I saw prisons with open doors for people to come out,
And I saw homes with open doors for people to enter in.

I saw beauty at every street corner
And heard music in every home.
I saw people discussing religion in bus queues,
And politics in the tube.
I saw babies on the knees of old men,
While their parents danced.

I saw green grass, free from litter,
And trees full of birds.

I heard people singing as they cleaned the pavements:
I saw houses, strong and shining with new paint.
I saw each family with a home of their own
And friends to share it.

I saw people free: to love and to be loved, to give
and to receive.
I saw peace in people's hearts, joy in people's eyes.
And a song on everyone's lips.
I saw dreams being dreamt
And lights shining in the darkness:
I saw water in the desert
And fire in the mountains:

I felt warmth in the winter-time
And heard laughter in the rain:
And I saw a pound note in the gutter
That nobody had bothered to pick up.

Yes, John, I am beginning to see the vision! Living in the twenty-first century on this island called planet earth, I am beginning to see your vision. God's vision. I can see us, all God's children, embracing and sitting down at the same table and looking each other in the eye in the presence of the one who calls each one of us "Beloved."
Amen and Amen!

11

Christ, the Inner Compass

Not that I have already obtained this or have already reached the goal; but I press on to make it my own, because Christ Jesus has made me his own. Beloved, I do not consider that I have made it my own; but this one thing I do: forgetting what lies behind and straining forward to what lies ahead, I press on toward the goal for the prize of the heavenly call of God in Christ Jesus. (Philippians 3:12-14)

It got to the place where enough was enough. I decided to take 1 Corinthians 6:19 seriously and not just reflect about it but live it. Yes, the apostle Paul's words were finally going to find some fertile ground in my life. When Paul asked me once again, "Do you not know that your body is a temple of the Holy Spirit within you, which you have from God, and that you are not your own?" I answered that I knew I was going to show it not just by doing good but by looking good. The doing good had always been easy. The looking good was going to take some hard work but I was going to do it all the same. I was going to lose the fat, drop the gut, tone up and slim down.

I got myself a personal trainer. In fact, I got two of them. One was a friend from church, the other was a pro at a health club in town. My

69

church friend was not technically "a personal trainer", but she was my hero nonetheless. Up in her sixties, she was active, the best cook I knew and she didn't look like fitness was a painful habit. Her name was Mary Jo Solie. She had a sweet, gentle face and said she would take me on as a swimming student free of charge. It sounded even better when the Y.W.C.A. gave me free use of their heated pool. Life was good. Well, it was until my trainer started talking about 7 a.m. starts and 10-lap sessions.

When you're the parent of a little baby, getting ready for 7 a.m. translates into waking up at three in the morning. But I was charged and ready and willing, so I bought myself my first swim suit and a cap to keep my braids dry. I was psyched, so much so that I went over to one of the health clubs in town and recruited personal trainer number two.

I asked him, "Can you make me look like you?" And he said, "Yes. You should have seen me when I looked like you!" Sign me up, I said. I paid an arm and a leg and then I went shopping for some serious exercise gear complete with a bandanna just like in the keep-fit videos. My first session was a shock. My personal trainer sat me down and gave me a lecture. A lecture! I didn't want a lecture, I wanted to pump iron.

After the lecture he gave me some reading to do and he talked about paperwork. I was to fill out a form and for two weeks I was to keep track of when, what and how I ate. It had to be detailed, including the kind and amount of salad dressing on my lettuce leaf and tomato slice. This was beginning to sound like serious work. My second session was rough. I got home wiped out and the next morning I couldn't move. I felt like I had been hit by a truck. And meanwhile, Mary Jo had stopped being Mrs. Nice Guy and was insisting that I let go of the side of the pool and venture into deep water. "You won't drown," she insisted, "I am here by your side, my dear." Yeah, right, famous last words. And I was beginning to realise that getting in shape was about more than having the right attitude and the right outfit; it was hard work.

Then one day I thought to myself, "I am paying to get hurt". So I said to my personal trainer, "I could do these things without you" and he said something amazing to me: "Yes, you could and when you get your inner compass you will not need me. When you get your inner compass you will choose to eat right and exercise all on your own."

That image of the inner compass says so much. In our spiritual lives an inner compass is what makes the difference between being religious and being spiritual. A religious person is a good person, someone who depends on the external compasses. And God has given us some wonderful external compasses such as Scripture, church, reason, the apostles and Jesus. In contrast, a spiritual person is one who has an inner compass.

Trouble occurs when we are not prepared to grow from being a religious person to a spiritual one, from being guided by an external compass to an internal one. We are so addicted to the external compasses that we give power over our spiritual lives to outside sources or external manifestations. Suddenly it is all about crossing the t's and dotting the i's and has very little to do with loving God or enjoying God's company, with finding our identity with God; knowing who we are, not through what we have or do not have but because each one of us is a child of God and nothing, absolutely nothing, can erase our baptism. If we depend too much on external compasses we become dysfunctional in our relationship with God and we imagine that God always owes us something. We assume that bad things can never happen to us. And when they do, we get mad at God. That dysfunctional spiritual orientation cannot survive the reality of the human journey because regardless of how good we are, life is filled with disappointments, betrayal, losses and grief.

To be religious is to do Spirituality 101 and stay there all your life. To be religious is a good start but you have to move on. The ancient Greek word for religious is ambiguous in meaning. It corresponds to a sort of cowardice with respect to the divine. It is classified alongside superstition. According to two of the ancient thinkers, Augustine and Plutarch, religiosity is worse than atheism, it is worse than total disbelief in God. The trouble with religion is that the external compasses can become an end and not a means. They become false Gods.

It is as crazy as driving from Green Bay to Chicago and running into a sign that says "Chicago" and you get out and pitch your tent by the sign thinking you have arrived. It might sound far-fetched but it happens so often in our spiritual lives. Take for instance when my dad asked me, "Before you leave Green Bay, are you going to visit the folks who stopped coming to church because you took over as pastor?" I was taken aback. I told him, "Dad, I have been praying for them but I am more concerned about the people who joined the church because they found my presence welcoming, because they found me to be a helpful pointer. I am concerned about those people because I want to make sure they know I am a signpost pointing to God, and should the signpost ever be renovated or replaced, it does not mean you abandon your journey."

You should never fall in love with the signpost and decide to pitch camp beside it, abandoning the journey altogether. And you should never leave a church or stop giving to God's work because a fellow member's actions or words anger or upset you. The church does not belong to any one person or group; it is a gift from God, it belongs to us all. I tell you, as a pastor I am encouraged to read the reasons people join our church. It is comforting to see that most of them say they join because of the people who attend.

Most of the time, thank God, the pressure is off the pastor. It is the people, the members, who attract others. One preacher said sheep beget sheep, a shepherd does not beget sheep. One of God's greatest desires is that one day there will be no need for an outside compass because people will have the law of God written in their hearts.

I don't know where you are on your journey but if you are a spiritual person, may God continue blessing you on the journey. If you are a religious person, don't give up, it's a good beginning but make sure you have not set up camp at a signpost whatever that signpost is or says. Jesus tells us he must leave so that the Holy Spirit can come. The Holy Spirit is the inner compass which writes the law of God so that we walk towards God even when it is pitch black, so that we know the direction coming from within us. May God grant that you and I, the church as a community, may always be faithful pointers to God. Amen.

12

Child of God

Now he was teaching in one of the synagogues on the sabbath. And just then there appeared a woman with a spirit that had crippled her for eighteen years. She was bent over and was quite unable to stand up straight. When Jesus saw her, he called her over and said, "Woman, you are set free from your ailment." When he laid his hands on her, immediately she stood up straight and began praising God. But the leader of the synagogue, indignant because Jesus had cured on the sabbath, kept saying to the crowd, "There are six days on which work ought to be done; come on those days and be cured, and not on the sabbath day." But the Lord answered him and said, "You hypocrites! Does not each of you on the sabbath untie his ox or his donkey from the manger, and lead it away to give it water? (Luke 13:10-15)

Holy time, holy space. That is the setting. The place is a synagogue and the time is a sabbath day. The day is among the holiest of days and the place is among the holiest of places. Sabbath: a serious day. "Remember the sabbath day, and keep it holy." (Exodus 20:8).

On such a day in such a place, we meet an unnamed woman. She pops out of the blue into Luke's story and arrests the eye of the Gospel reader. We don't know much about her. We are not told her name, her hometown or whether she has family or not. We know nothing about her except that she is in a synagogue on a sabbath day and she has a medical condition. Her ailment is not a private affair; it can be observed by all. She is crippled to the point of being bent over double. Something is destroying her from the inside out. And it had been gnawing away at her for a long, long time: 18 years. Either way you count it, 18 years is a long time to be unable to stand up straight. A baby born in the first month of the crippled woman's affliction would now not only be walking, talking and dating, but would be packing to leave home for college or might even be getting married.

Eighteen years is a long time. Some would say it is long enough for you to stop believing that you are ever going to get well. So it is surprising that we meet the woman not on the roadside begging and not in her bed curled up wishing she were dead, but in a place of worship. And fortunately for her, on that day, God was present not only in the written word but in the person of Jesus. Watch out, someone is going to get strengthened from the inside out!

The modern reader might guess at the woman's condition as arthritis or osteoporosis. Not so for Luke, for whom all life is read with a theological lens. The gospel speaks of her condition as a spiritual matter: she had a spirit of weakness or, in some translations, of infirmity. Her affliction had attacked the very core of her being. No matter how hard she tried, she could not straighten herself. It was an affliction that had disfigured her, dehumanized her. She could no longer walk upright. She had collapsed from the inside out and no matter how hard she tried, she could not straighten herself up.

And some might wonder, "Who is this bent-over woman?" Could she, in a literal sense, be one of the many women in Africa, who live day by day almost doubled up under the burden of a child on her back or bent-over working a patch of land with a hoe? Or is she as literal as the many women in Africa doubled up under a load of firewood on her head and a pail of water in her hand?

Then it happened on a sabbath day in the synagogue that a holy man's eyes saw her. And not only did Jesus see her, he acted by calling her. He moved her from the periphery and into the limelight. After 18 years she was no longer invisible. She became the main story on that holy day in that holy place. Her healing became the only item on the agenda.

Bent over double, her eyes were always on the ground when she walked. Her world was made up of things you see when you look down: the dust, the pavement, feet, shoes, trash. Her world was without blue sky, clouds, moon, stars or faces. She did not see very far, she saw just the next step she would take. She was literally near-sighted, not as a result of poor eyesight but because her posture prevented her from seeing anything other than the ground.

Her suffering had stretched from the first month of her attack through 18 long years. Much had happened between the time she doubled up and the day she met Jesus. It had been such a long time that nobody remembered her being any other way. Maybe they had even forgotten that she could be any other way. But I don't think she ever got used to being bent double; there are things one can never get used to.

When our eyes fall on God's world, we see this condition of being bent double. Our world seems to have been taken hostage by some evil spirit. The newscasts are often a litany of bad news. In some places this has been going on for so long that some think it will never change. After so many years of crisis and disaster, some are even used to living in that kind of a world. There is a short-sightedness associated with such a worldview and it calls for a straightening up.

One of my favorite stories best comments on this condition. The story is told of an eagle's egg that found its way into a chicken's nest. Mother hen hatched her eggs and among them she unknowingly hatched an eagle. That little eaglet thought she was a chicken. Sure did! After all, her mother was a chicken, her brothers and sisters were chickens, and she thought she was a chicken. And so she learned all the things that chickens do. She learned how to scratch around and make a living out of keeping her eye on the ground.

Story says, there came a day when a beautiful big eagle was flying around and almost smashed into a tree—could hardly believe her eyes to see the little "chicken-eagle" who was down below scratching around madly. The big eagle perched on a tree to look closely. And after taking as much of it as she could, because indeed it is painful to watch an eagle scratch around like a chicken, the big eagle called out "Pssstttt!"

The little eaglet looked up and said, "Who me?"

"Yes you!" said big eagle. "What are you doing scratching around?"

"I am a chicken," said little eaglet. "That's what we do."

"You are not a chicken!" exclaimed big eagle.

"Yes I am," replied eaglet.

"No you are not."

"Yes I am"

"Not."

"I am."

"Not."

"I am."

That went on almost the entire morning until big eagle said, "Stretch out your wings!" Little eaglet stretched her wings and she could hardly believe she had wings that spread far beyond any chicken's wings.

"Flap!" said big eagle.

And little eaglet flapped and flapped and flapped. And as she flapped she began to rise and rise and rise and soon she was soaring. Oh my! All these years and she did not know she could fly.

This story could be about Jesus who came to remind us who we are and to free us from the things that would cripple us, keep us bent double with shame or anger or fear, keeping us with our eyes fixed on the ground. Jesus came to call us to stretch, to grow, to stand up straight, to soar. Child of God, you are called for no less than this. This is your day to fly.

An Interview with Preachers and Teachers from the United States, Africa and Europe

David Hay Jones talks about preaching with Dr. Eddie Fox, Rev. Cynthia Johnson-Oliver, Professor Liv Berit Carlsen, Rev. Annette-Grace Zimondi, Rev. Bill Barnes and Mr. Stu Smith.

David Hay Jones: At its best, I think good preaching turns "a parched land into springs of water" (Psalm 107:35). Which Bible verse do you think best defines preaching and its role?

Dr. Eddie Fox: For me, it is when the psalmist declares, "Let the redeemed of the Lord say so…" (Psalm 107:2).

Rev. Cynthia Johnson-Oliver: I would choose, "The lion has roared; who will not fear? The Lord God has spoken; who can but prophesy?" (Amos 3:8).

Liv Berit Carlsen: I think of, "While they were talking and discussing, Jesus himself came near and went with them" (Luke, 24: 15).

David Hay Jones: To begin with basics, what exactly is preaching and why is there a need for it?

Dr. Eddie Fox: Preaching matters! Preaching is both the expectation of God and the desperate need for God in today's world. The first act of God in creation was that God spoke. God spoke and creation happened. When a person is preaching the good news of Christ

Jesus, there is nothing more important. Dr. William E. Sangster wrote, "On one's way to preach the gospel the most modest person may whisper, 'Nothing more important will happen in this town this week than the work I am doing now.' " ("Power in Preaching", Abingdon, p. 21). The time is right for the preaching of the Gospel of the Lord Jesus Christ.

To preach the Gospel, the good news of Christ Jesus, means the following: "To proclaim the biography of the deeds of God in terms of one's autobiography with the hope that persons, enabled by the power of the Holy Spirit, respond to God's act of forgiveness in Jesus Christ, in repentance and faith, and live out the new life in faithfulness to the kingdom of God." ("Let the Redeemed of the Lord Say So!" by Fox and Morris).

Preaching is God's idea. God is self-disclosing; God calls people to declare his marvelous works and grace for all persons. It is not our idea that we enter into this business of preaching. God is a missionary God who calls and sends forth God's messengers with the good news of God's kingdom.

Rev. Cynthia Johnson-Oliver: In his famous "I have a dream speech", Dr. Martin Luther King, Jr. spoke of the nation's circumstance as one in which America had defaulted on a promissory note by promising life, liberty and the pursuit of happiness and instead rendering segregation, poverty and racial injustice. Yet, he had a vision of a future in which the sons of former slaves and the sons of former slave owners would be able to sit down together at a table of brotherhood. In this speech, Dr. King demonstrated a profound and poignant understanding of the present as well as a radical vision, until then unimaginable, about America's future. The power of this vision reverberated in dual directions: it moved some people to risk their lives, while it moved others to take the lives of civil rights activists. Nevertheless, it is this combination of a unique insight into the present and a radical vision of the future that is, in my view, the essence of prophetic preaching.

Prophetic preaching is one of the oldest forms of preaching in the Judeo-Christian traditions. Prophecy bookmarks some of Israel's most troubling historical periods, from the bold declarations of Elijah in the Northern Kingdom to the messianic hopes of Second Isaiah during the Babylonian exile. The office of prophet was reaffirmed in the early Christian community in the Epistle to the Ephesians 4:11, "The gifts he gave were that some would be apostles, some prophets, some evangelists, some pastors and teachers." I believe that from this five-fold ministry there are correspondingly five types of preaching: apostolic, prophetic, evangelistic, pastoral, and instructional. Prophetic preaching, however, is often overlooked in contemporary Christianity.

By prophetic preaching, I mean preaching that displays divinely inspired wisdom or knowledge about the present and/or the future. It may not necessarily include the foretelling of future events, but certainly it is forth-telling, that is, a proclamation that is forward-looking in time, place or order. It could be wisdom about what is to come if a community continues on a certain path or a vision of what could be if another course of action is taken. The prophetic preacher possesses at least three traits: a strong compelling need to deliver a message, a radical commitment to the message no matter the cost, and the ability to be change-agents in their community because of their message.

David Hay Jones: Please expand on these three qualities of the prophetic preacher.

Rev. Cynthia Johnson-Oliver: First, while almost all preaching is preceded by "the call," there is something unique about the urgency with which the prophet proclaims the word of God. Amos describes prophecy as the only imaginable response when the Lord God has spoken. Indeed, it is as logical and as necessary a response as fearing the roar of a lion. Jeremiah, in his fifth personal lament (20:7-13), speaks of a burning fire deep in his bones to proclaim his message, despite all of the danger and hatred that his prophetic words of warning inspired. Prophetic preaching might require a strong compelling need because of the serious responsibility placed on the prophet. Ezekiel 33:6 describes this responsibility as that of a sentinel, "But if the sentinel sees the sword coming and does not blow the trumpet, so that the people are not warned, and the sword comes and takes any of them…their blood I will require at the sentinel's hand." The passage goes on to describe Ezekiel as a sentinel for the house of Israel, required to deliver words of warning from the mouth of God to the people.

Second, because they are compelled, prophets also possess a radical commitment to the truth of their message. They boldly speak truth to power in the tradition of Jeremiah, and refuse to alter their message to make it more palatable. Moreover, whether willing (Isaiah 6:8) or unwilling (Jonah 1:3), whether prophesying good news (Isaiah 40-55) or destruction (Jeremiah), the prophet is committed to the message despite its consequences. Dr. King, in his mountaintop speech, spoke of his desire to live a long life. He proclaimed, "Longevity has its place. But I'm not concerned about that now. I just want to do God's will." While Dr. King willingly risked his life, not all prophets are called upon to take this ultimate risk. However, they may risk popularity and status, or may simply gain enemies or discomfit friends because of the message. This willingness to persist, despite the consequences, is the hallmark of the prophet.

Finally, the prophet, in being compelled and radically committed to proclaiming the message, is a change-agent in the community that witnesses the message. Jonah inspired communal repentance in Ninevah to avoid the outcome of his prophecy. Amos called upon his community to trade their vain celebrations and to instead "let justice roll down like waters, and righteousness like an ever-flowing stream." Similarly, Dr. King inspired change in the hearts and minds of Americans, an accomplishment that not even the legal mandates of the Supreme Court could achieve. In sum, the community that receives the prophetic message is changed by it—for the better if they accept the prophecy or for the worse if they reject the warning.

Rev. Annette Grace Zimondi: The twenty-first century church needs prophetic preaching that is liberating and empowering, a kind of preaching that presents God not as a judging figure but as a loving parent, a type of preaching that engages and is relevant to children, youth and adults and leaves the heart "strangely warmed". The preacher's task is to remind us of God's point of view, but more than that, calls us to action and community building. As a prophet, the preacher depends on God for her task and is empowered by God.

As soon as a great preacher stands up to deliver the word, you can read in her eyes that she is a prophet charged with the task of liberation and empowerment. The sermon's introduction is critical. It should state the theme of the sermon in a powerful way: "The last things first." The introduction should be appetizing, letting the hearers know from the beginning that they are about to walk a fascinating spiritual journey with the preacher. The preacher does not walk alone in her preaching. Under the guidance of the Holy Spirit, she walks with her congregation.

The preacher should deliver the word of God clearly and to the point. She should be able to engage the congregation by her use of profound thought and sense of humor. In addition, the preacher's life makes her an example and worth listening to. The preacher's life is therefore a powerful sermon.

Liv Berit Carlsen: Worship and sermons are crucial to teach, equip, and encourage Christians to live authentic and courageous lives. The sermon has to be presented in words that open the hearer's mind. Preaching describes a life where our faith is like a landscape which includes the whole and true life. In preaching, there is a dialogue between experiences and insights.

David Hay Jones: Professor Carlsen, as a Scandinavian Christian you live in a society where most people do not attend church regularly. How do you make Christianity relevant to unchurched people?

Liv Berit Carlsen: Fewer and fewer postmodern men and women go to church, yet men and women are longing for somebody, or something, to believe in, somebody to follow and somebody to pray to. Many men and women do not know where to go, whom to follow or how to pray. In my opinion, Christ is not the problem. I have come more and more to believe that modern men and women read the Christian's daily life as a sermon. Christians do not have more power or knowledge than anyone else. So preaching should not just be in words but in the daily life of a believer, which can have great impact on the believer's surroundings.

In my home country, Norway, I believe the term fellow traveler, or fellow wanderer, expresses values and norms that unchurched people all over the world are longing and looking for. To be a fellow traveler means to stand by or next to someone, not opposite or over them. Fellow-traveling in the faith landscape is characterized by openness, self-disclosure and even curiosity. Such faith conversations invite men and women into a space where we can wonder and reflect together. As pastors and deacons we are challenged to share our experiences as fellow travelers. We find our model in the story about the walk to Emmaus. Without their knowing it, Christ himself was their fellow wanderer or traveler. "While they were talking and discussing, Jesus himself came near and went with them ..." (Luke, 24:15).

This was true for me a few weeks ago. During an Alpha course where I taught how to talk about our Christian faith, I shared a story of how our family had been shaken one evening after our daughter had been escorted home by the local police. The owner of a little café nearby had grown tired of rebellious youngsters there and had phoned the police and told them that our daughter Cecilie was the most active of the rowdy youngsters. After the police left, we invited the group of youngsters to our house in order to listen to their story and share our fears and anger.

When I finished my little sermon, several in the Alpha group responded, some with tears because they recalled similar situations in their own lives. Others expressed relief at learning of our real life experience. The dialogue which followed was surprisingly open, touching and filled with warmth. Weeks later I learned that sharing our little family crisis—especially considering we are a Christian family—had opened the ears and hearts of unchurched friends in the Alpha group. The life we live can be our most effective sermon.

Stu Smith: I would like to deal with the question of good preaching by approaching it differently from the previous commentators.

I want to answer the question, "What makes a perfect preacher?" For me, the perfect preacher must be three things: an actor with style and technique; a storyteller for voicing unforgettable images; and a magician who can pull spiritual surprises out of the theological hat.

A perfect preacher rejects liturgical and biblical cliches and stretches our imaginations with fresh interpretations of the time-worn and all-too-familiar. I would banish petty, personal stories from the pulpit—save them for the dinner table! The exception would be those stories that reach beyond the maudlin into something universally meaningful.

As an actor, my perfect preacher would know the power of the pause and when to add dramatic dynamics to what's being said.

As a storyteller, my perfect preacher would tell stories, not read them, creating an unblinking connection between pulpit and pew.

As a magician, my preacher would dare to turn old stories into fresh ones, offering ideas that risk being outisde the box (the one the Bible came in). My ideal preacher would get me listening instead of hearing, thinking instead of snoozing. I want to be spiritually surprised and energized.

That's what I look for in a perfect pastor and preacher: a new battery for my old flashlight, a flickering flame in a dark head.

David Hay Jones: You all have personal experience of Grace Imathiu's preaching. Please tell us about her special qualities as a preacher and Bible study leader.

Dr. Eddie Fox: Rev. Grace Imathiu is one who has clearly heard God's call to be a forth-teller of the Gospel. She understands that we have been given a message to proclaim. When one hears Grace preach, one hears the word of God. She proclaims the "biography of the deeds of God." To listen to Grace preach and teach is to hear the words of the Holy Scripture come to life and become living words of faith and hope. The content of the message is the heart of the matter.

Sir Alan Walker often remarked, "What shall it profit the church if it perfects its technique and discovers that it has nothing to say." Well, the Christian Church has a message and the good news is Christ Jesus. When Grace preaches, one listens. She declares "good news of the kingdom of God."

And in Grace, the message can be seen as well as heard. She speaks in such a way that the story of the Gospel connects through her story with the listener's story and invites a response to the good news. Her message is invitational. Through the power of the Holy Spirit the message demands response and graciously invites the hearer to receive hope, healing and salvation in the name of Jesus. Receiving the gift of storytelling through her family and culture, Grace has the gracious gift of helping a person see and experience the story of the Gospel in the present moment. I have heard Grace speak in many different settings, to many different ages, many different cultures and many languages, and always she communicates the good news of Jesus through her message. For Grace, her very being enables one to see the message and respond in faith through the power of the Holy Spirit.

I am really happy that my colleague and friend, Grace Imathiu has put these messages in print. Each person who reads these messages of hope will be encouraged and inspired to follow Jesus. No preacher ever stands alone, for we are always surrounded by those who believe in us and those who stand with us. Grace has been "graced" through her family, her friends and her many experiences around the entire world and now many persons will receive grace through the messages of hope.

By grace, we are a part of a new kingdom with a new hope. We have received salvation in Christ and we are all called to be ambassadors of Christ in a world that so desperately needs salvation. Grace has given us a marvelous example and great encouragement to be a witness and an ambassador of the Lord Jesus Christ. We praise God that we do have something to say! We stake our very life on the conviction that God did in fact come in human form in Christ Jesus to redeem and restore creation, including all people everywhere. What a message. Surely we, like Grace Imathiu, are compelled to say so. And through the power of the Holy Spirit we are given power and confidence to say so.

Rev. Cynthia Johnson-Oliver: I believe that many of Grace Imathiu's sermons possess the characteristics of prophetic preaching. I remember a sermon that she preached at an international Methodist event. In the sermon, she compared Joseph's meeting with his estranged brothers in Genesis to intercontinental race relations between Africans and Americans. Joseph had been sold into slavery by his brothers but later rose to prominence in Egypt. When there was famine throughout the region, his brothers had to appeal to him for food. However, they did not recognize Joseph at first. Grace appealed to the audience using the words of Joseph, "Come closer to me. I am your sister." She called upon us to shed our notions of American uniqueness and cultural separation from "the other" and recognize that the person standing in front of us is no stranger, but in fact our long, lost brother/sister. Her message, if truly received, could change the perspective of American church and society as we encounter other people: we may one day need our brother, and hopefully he will not still be angry about how we have treated him.

Grace's sermons and other prophetic messages reveal that prophetic preaching still has a place in contemporary Christianity. Indeed, one does not have to reach Dr. King's prominence nor even be called upon to make a similar sacrifice to be a prophetic preacher. Prophets are needed in pulpits large and small and on platforms national and local. Churches and societies need people unafraid to tell the truth about our present and proffer a vision for the future. We need prophets who are willing to make us uncomfortable enough with the present that we become compelled to create a new future. There is still a need for prophets who will speak the truth no matter the costs. Prophets for whom popularity is not a primary concern. Prophets who dare to turn a mirror on our churches, our communities, and our world, and cause us to see ourselves as we really are. These compelled, committed, change-agents are necessary for us to move from where we are to where we ought to be. "The Lord has spoken; who can but prophesy?"

Rev. Annette Grace Zimondi: Grace Imathiu is one of the few preachers able to interpret the word of God and make it relevant to all ages and backgrounds. Without a doubt, her expertise in exegesis, her international experience and her humor have equipped her as fascinating preacher. After you hear her preach, you wish she had not stopped because she leaves you wanting to hear more.

Liv Berit Carlsen: Our challenge in the sermon and in preaching is to let dialogue occur with our fellow travelers. In her preaching, Grace Imathiu is able to allow dialogue to occur with her fellow traveler as she shares not only words but also her Christian experience.

Rev. Bill Barnes: When I heard Grace Imathiu deliver her Bible study and sermons at the World Methodist Conference in Rio de Janeiro in 1996, something rare was occurring for me. Her words were charged and generated by a spirit and I knew something holy and eternal was coming at me. As I opened more and more to that spirit, the "at" was coming 'into" me, and I knew that it was surely moving "through" me as well, empowering mind and feet and hands into healing. For me, that is the highest tribute I can pay to preaching. Grace Imathiu is graciously blessed with that power, a blessing rare in my opinion.

Surely some of that power is attributable to another truth about her: word and deed are melded perfectly in her life. The inclusiveness and universality, as well as the humor and simplicity, in her preaching are marvelously lived out in her ministry, in her family and friends, and in her personal decisions. For years I have benefited from Grace's sermonic gifts and from the exemplary integrity of her life. Therefore, it is truly a joy to recall how thankful and blessed I am by Grace.

Stu Smith: Grace was the great awakening for us in the comfortable pews of a large, all-white, inner-city church in Green Bay, Wisconsin.

From the very first moment, she startled us with her presence, the theological ingenuity of her sermons, her treasure trove of Kenyan stories, the spontaneity of her laughter and the radiant joy of her commitment to God. Grace's arms encircle the world. We heard that in her sermons. We felt that in our lives. We will never be the same, and for that we're forever grateful.

David Hay Jones: Thank you to everyone who participated here with their wise words about preaching and its role and relevance today. I am sure that this interview will become a useful resource to students of preaching everywhere.

Notes on the contributors

Rev. Cynthia Johnson-Oliver is an ordained elder in the Christian Methodist Episcopal Church. She is a fifth generation preacher and the granddaughter of the late Bishop Joseph A. Johnson, Jr. of the C.M.E. Church. She is a graduate of Harvard College magna cum laude (B.A., Comparative Religion), Harvard Divinity School (M.T.S.), and Yale Law School (J.D.). She currently serves as Connectional Director of Youth Ministry for the C.M.E. Church.

Rev. Bill Barnes is the founder of Edgehill U.M.C., Nashville, Tennessee, the first integrated congregation in the city. He served there for 30 years. When Rev. Barnes retired as pastor of Edgehill U.M.C., Nashville city officials proclaimed Sunday, June 2, 1996 as "Reverend Bill Barnes Day in Nashville" to honor his service.

Rev. Annette Grace Zimondi is a citizen of Zimbabwe, an ordained minister of the Zimbabwe Methodist Church and a graduate student at Vanderbilt University, Nashville.

Liv Berit Carlsen, an ordained deacon, is assistant to the bishop of the United Methodist Church, Nordic and Baltic Episcopal Area. She is an assistant professor of nursing and the author of two books on nursing. She lives near Oslo, Norway.

Dr. Eddie Fox, Nashville, is Director of Evangelism for the World Methodist Council.

Mr. Stu Smith is an advertising consultant, actor, storyteller, singer, son of O.B. Smith (to whom this book is dedicated), and a 30-year member of First United Methodist Church, Green Bay, Wisconsin.

A Conversation with R. Grace Imathiu and Readers of her Website

Grace, please describe your childhood in Kenya. Tell us where you were born and grew up.

I was born in the town of Meru in Kenya. Meru lies smack dab on the equator and I like to call it "the belly button" of the planet. It is a very fertile place where anything will grow: tea, coffee, mango, papaya, passion fruit, as well as familiar vegetables such as beans, onions and potatoes.

Meru is close to Mount Kenya, one of Africa's highest mountains, with snowy peaks way up high in the clouds. Meru town is in the foothills, about 8000 feet above sea level. It is a warm place if you compare it with, say, winter in Wisconsin and yet it's cool and dry if you compare it with summer in Wisconsin. I remember as a child thinking the sky in Meru was an incredible, mesmerizing deep blue; I am fortunate to have been born in such a beautiful part of the world.

My father was a prominent pastor and my mother was a teacher. In fact, up until I was nine, my father was my pastor at church and my mother was my english and geography teacher at school.

When I was about three, my parents traveled to England for further studies and my sister, brother and I stayed in Kenya and were looked after by our grandparents and relatives.

I treasure those early childhood memories of growing up in my grandmother's house. I was surrounded by love.

What was it like being born into a professional church family? Your father is a bishop and your mother a lay preacher; it sounds like being a Christian was natural for you from the very beginning.

Being a Christian was as natural as being from the Meru tribe or being a human being. It was true for everybody I knew and there was no question about the reality, existence or love of God for the world. Our central text in Sunday School and in our services was John 3:16: "For God so loved the world that he gave his only Son". In my mind, God's love would pursue us and sacrifice everything for us; God's becoming a human in Jesus Christ showed that clearly. God's love was a hounding, unremitting, unrelenting love. It was to this God that I responded and I remember growing up with a passion for God. I think I spent three-quarters of my childhood in church. And I loved it.

As you know it is not unusual, especially in Europe, for people not to attend church at all. Your childhood situation was quite the opposite. Did you ever risk getting burned out on church?

Of course not. I grew up wishing every day was Sunday. Church was the best thing that happened to us each week. The ground was leveled on that Sunday morning. No matter who you were and what you owned, once you got into church, worldly wealth did not matter. So those with stylish suits sat next to those with no shoes, those with doctorates sat next to those who did not know how to read and write. What mattered was that this was God's space and God's time and God was in charge.

The worship services were not dull one-man shows which were neatly scripted with the preacher in charge of everything while we all sat bored and quiet in the pews. No sir! We were all participants, making the worship service work and happen. So, if we got to singing a hymn and it was dragging along or was dull, someone in the congregation would go to the front of the church, stop the show and we would either have to start again and sing with some zest and vigor or we would change the hymn. And then the different groups in the church would have their moment to shine and they would compete with each other: the youth choir, the children's choir, the women's choir, the men's choir, the church choir, special groups, short dramas and skits.

The reading of Scripture was always an exciting moment. To start with, our language is very difficult to read. I don't quite know how to explain it; there are some sounds in our language that cannot seem to find a way to be nailed down in written language. So when the Scriptures were being read, there would almost always be a word that would have the reader stumped. So he or she would stop mid-sentence and ask for help.

"People," the reader would ask, "who knows how to pronounce this word?" Of course, a whole bunch of voices in the congregation would respond with a whole bunch of different pronunciations. And then maybe someone would ask, "What does that word mean? I have never heard it before." And somebody would get up and explain the meaning. And often someone else would get up and either add to what had been said or give a completely different meaning. It was living church.

Church was wonderful in a world without television. The community gathered in church not only for inspiration and to worship God but also for information and entertainment. The fact that we are church folk does not mean we stop being real people involved in the real world. Unfortunately, some church folk are so heavenly bound, they are no earthly good.

Growing up in this safe and loving environment, can you recall grappling with theological questions? What issues or problems did you wonder about?

I can recall a couple of theological moments. The first was when I was about six. My father was away at a huge evangelism rally in some remote part of our region. Our baby brother Timothy was rushed to hospital. My father must have come back later that night. What I remember clearly was seeing my parents' car as I walked to school early the next morning and I was so surprised and happy to see them I rushed madly across the field, got to the road and was waving wildly. But for the first time in my life, they did not seem to see me. My mother was crying and my father was looking the way he looks when he whistles a hymn. I spent the day in school quite confused. Later that day I learned that Timothy had died. I think it was pneumonia. And at that moment I realized that just because God loved us and we loved God, it did not mean we were immune from the bad things that happened to people. For the longest time after Timothy's death I had all kinds of nightmares, trying to find a new way to understand what being loved and loving God meant. I don't think I figured it out. I think it eventually got overtaken by other stuff like grades and our moving to the capital city of Nairobi.

And the other theological incident?

My second early theological moment was when I was eight and wanted to attend what was known as "catechism classes". These were weekly classes for people who wanted to join the church. They were taught by a man I adored called Samson. He used to cut the thick hedges at our home. He was one of the first Christians in Meru. He never told his own story but folks would whisper it now and again.

He was a survivor of "The Fire", when the first 12 boys in the Christian school had been trapped in their dormitory room, the door latched from the outside, and the house set on fire. Samson still had the scars. He had almost died because of his faith. When I was eight, Samson seemed ancient history to me; he must have been about 60 or so. I couldn't wait to attend the classes he taught but one had to be at least 12-years-old.

After my relentless begging, the church finally said I could attend but I was not allowed to either talk or miss any class. Of course I would not be confirmed until I was 12. The first day in class was a theological moment when Samson looked around and asked the class, "Who is God?" Well, I had never ever thought to ask that. I had always assumed that everybody knew who God was. I didn't even know how I could respond to that question. But before I could think any further, everybody began to recite the answer they had learned by rote from the catechism book: "Murungu ni Baba wetu uria uri Iguru." (God is our Father who is in heaven.) The catechism book had all the answers, but I left class wondering what MY answer would be. I look back and really know I was blessed and privileged to have Samson as my first teacher of theology.

With all that "catechism" from Samson in your hair, you must have found it quite easy to become a full member of your local church.

Not really. When I was finally 12-years-old, it was time to formerly join the church. We had our confirmation class and then the night before the event, I announced to my parents I would not be confirmed because I was not ready.

My parents flipped. You see, I had really been a model Christian. In addition, my father was then Presiding Bishop of the Methodist Church in Kenya and my mother was the President of the Methodist Women's Movement. The family situation dictated that I would be confirmed, ready or not. So when I announced that I was not ready, my distraught parents called the pastor and he came over to have "a conversation" with me.

Did the pastor convince you?

I told the pastor I was not ready because I still had some questions that had not been addressed or the answers had not been convincing. He asked me what those questions were and I remember he did not answer them but told me that they were very good questions. Then he went on to explain that joining the church did not mean you had everything worked out. You continued to work on the questions as a member of the community of faith. So I formally joined the church with the permission to ask questions, wonder and ponder.

Grace, you are a world-renowned preacher. Which preachers and writers have inspired you to find your voice as a preacher?

Not all my favorite preachers have been published. I am especially aware of this when I think of African preachers, whose work it is to preach not write. My father Bishop Lawi Imathiu is one of my favorite preachers. In the past 30 years he has been one of the most influential people in Kenya, not just in the church but in politics, and yet he has not been published. A book of his sermons is long overdue. And we have to find a publisher for his memoirs. So much of the history of Methodism in Kenya is wrapped up in my father's life.

Of the preachers who are published, I especially like Renita Weems, Dr. Martin Luther King, Jr., Fred Craddock, Paul Tillich, Gardner C. Taylor and Barbara Brown Taylor. And I love the clear and simple language of Ted Loder's poetry.

Different preachers have taught me about different aspects of preaching. For example, Fred Craddock and Frederick Buechner are great storytellers and I have learnt from them how to structure a story. Paul Tillich has taught me how to preach from a firm theological ground. Dr. King, Bishop Desmond Tutu and Renita Weems have inspired me to be passionate about social justice.

Do you draw inspiration from prose and poetry?

Poems rather than novels feed into my sermons. I thrive on Adrienne Rich, Audre Lorde, Ted Loder, Gardner C. Taylor and Janice Mirikitani. These are writers who make me realise how beautiful language can be. They make me search for the best words with which to describe the Holy. For my own devotional life I read the Psalms and Song of Songs, Scripture's poetry.

I am a Bible scholar and I find the work of great thinkers to be a constant source of inspiration. My reading goes beyond biblical studies to philosophy, cultural studies and linguistics. I enjoy Gayatri Chakravorty Spivak, who writes on post-colonialism, Frantz Fanon, Karen Armstrong, Cornel West, and recently I have been dipping into the works of the linguist George Lakoff.

The daily newspaper is also a good source of sermon material, and with the internet I can access newspapers all over the world. I can keep in touch with my family and what's happening in Africa, Europe and America.

Conversations with my husband constantly filter into my sermons. He's an avid reader of short stories and novels and his enthusiasm for Virginia Woolf, John Cheever, Richard Yates and Raymond Carver can prod my thoughts into some unexpected and exciting nooks and crannies.

What would your advice be to a gifted young preacher about to take over as lead pastor of a church?

I would tell the person to find ways of making time for studying, think-ing, and wrestling with the word of God. You have to make time because no one will give it to you. Preaching is creative work like writing a book or painting a picture. The preparation doesn't always look like work to an outside observer. But it's demanding nevertheless: the struggle to find the right words, how to combine them, how to make scholarship meaningful and accessible to people. So my best advice is, find or make time and use it effectively.

Why not be a fulltime preacher traveling the world?

I am a disciple of Christ and preaching is the gift that I bring to the community of faith. By being involved in the work of community-building, I am seen and treated as a genuine human being, not a celebrity preacher or a pretend person constructed in people's minds. Hit-and-run preaching is too easy. I don't want to parachute in on people's lives and be flown out a few hours later. As a pastor, I am deeply involved in the congregation's spiritual struggles and growth. Building community is everything for me.

Finally, why does preaching matter?

That is the most important question I ask myself every week as I prepare the sermon. And my answer has always been a resounding "Yes! Preaching matters." I preach in order to believe and I believe because I preach. I invite my congregation to eavesdrop on my struggle to make that which is of utmost meaning, the word of God, matter in my daily life. Preaching builds community. It is as though we are on the witness stand, giving evidence of God's active presence in the world.

Publisher's information

"Words of Fire, Spirit of Grace" is the first in a series of Christian and inspirational books by True North Publishing.

For information about Grace Imathiu's second collection of sermons, David Hay Jones' "Beneath a Canopy of Leaves" and other books in our publishing program, please contact us at True North, Box 65, 982 60 Porjus, Sweden.

You can always reach us by email at dhayjones@yahoo.com, g47@mailcity.com and yougrace@lycos.com. You are encouraged to contact all three email addresses.